GO WILD!

101 THINGS TO DO OUTDOORS BEFORE YOU GROW UP

Fiona Danks and Jo Schofield

FRANCES LINCOLN LIMITED

PUBLISHERS

FOR CONNIE, DAN, EDWARD, HANNAH AND JAKE

Frances Lincoln Ltd
4 Torriano Mews
Torriano Avenue
London NW5 2RZ
www.franceslincoln.com
www.goingwild.net

Go Wild!
Copyright © Frances Lincoln 2009
Text copyright © Fiona Danks and Jo Schofield 2009
Photographs copyright © Jo Schofield and Fiona Danks 2009

First Frances Lincoln edition: 2009

Fiona Danks and Jo Schofield have asserted their right to be
identified as the authors of this work in accordance with the
Copyright, Designs and Patents Act 1988 (UK).

A catalogue record for this book is available from the British Library.

ISBN 978-0-7112-2939-6

Designed by Sarah Slack

Printed and bound in Singapore

9 8 7 6 5 4 3

**This book contains some potentially dangerous activities. Please note
that any readers, or anyone in their charge, taking part in any of the
activities described does so at their own risk. YOU MUST therefore follow
the commonsense SAFETY TIPS which appear throughout the book.
Neither the authors nor the publisher can accept any legal responsibility
for any harm, injury, damage, loss or prosecution resulting from the
activities described.**

**It is illegal to carry out any of these activities on private land without the
owner's permission, and there are laws relating both to the protection of
land, property, plants and animals, and to the use of weapons.**

CONTENTS

GO WILD 8

SHELTER 14
Shelters from natural materials 18
Tarpaulin shelters 22
The DIY tent 24
Tree houses 26
Igloos and snow shelters 28
How to go wild camping 30
Other ways of wild camping 33
Camping under a roof 34

FIRE 36
Being prepared 40
Making a good fire 44
Fire without matches 48
Fire essentials 53

FORAGING 54
Edible wild plants 58
Fungus foray and feast 61
Coastal foraging 64
Line fishing 66
Crayfishing 72
Wild meat 73

COOKING OUTDOORS 76
The basics 80
Cooking methods 82
Basic recipes for easy outdoor meals 85

TOOLS & WEAPONS 90
Tool safety and use 94
Stone Age tools 97
Catapults 99
Natural missile launchers 101

Bows and arrows 104

Peashooters 108

Blowpipes 109

Making your own bushcraft knife 110

BUSHCRAFT SKILLS 112

Wooden tools and implements 116

Natural cordage 120

A few useful knots 121

Lashing cord to make
camp furniture 125

WATER & KEEPING CLEAN 126

Water know-how 130

Keeping a clean camp 134

Wilderness toilets 137

KEEPING SAFE 140

Equipment 144

Bushcraft first-aid kit 147

Natural remedies 148

FURTHER INFORMATION 152

Finding your way 154

Finding your way without a map 155

Leaving no trace 156

Discovering more about bushcraft 156

Index 158

Acknowledgements 160

GO WILD

They lay watching the ever-changing scene in front of them, completely absorbed and totally at ease with their surroundings. These thirteen-year-old boys weren't lounging on the sofa in front of the TV: they were deep in the woods, lying on the ground staring into the heart of a fire. And this wasn't just any old fire: it was their very own fire, made by striking flint against steel, built on a cleared area on the forest floor from wood they had gathered.

All around them were their shelters; some of them had strung hammocks between trees, some had made simple tents from tarpaulins, others had made natural shelters using sticks and leaves. They had dug a latrine pit, carved rustic spoons and tent pegs, and cooked bread dough on sticks. Now it was time to lie back and relax in the darkening forest, with only the screech of owls and the crackle of the fire to disturb the peace. This was their day and night of going wild, of escaping into the great outdoors and learning something about the rudiments of bushcraft. It was perhaps the highlight of their summer holidays, a memory that will stay with them forever.

Most young people can navigate expertly through two-dimensional virtual worlds but are completely disconnected from the reality of the great outdoors. Some have so little experience of all things natural that they are disgusted by mud, squeamish about little creatures or even frightened of raw elements like the wind. Many have never experienced simple pleasures such as sitting round a campfire, sleeping outdoors or whittling a stick. You could argue that technology is their future; when they can order everything they desire, even designer shoes, on the Internet, why on earth do they need to know about finding food, making shelter or building fire? But we believe that when children and teenagers experience a touch of wildness and learn basic outdoor skills it increases their self-confidence and encourages free thinking and environmental awareness.

We believe too that young people – in fact everyone – need to reconnect with the natural world: touch it, feel it, taste it, play in it, sleep in it. Wild places ease the stresses and strains of modern life, providing a sense of freedom and exuberance. Yet we are increasingly motivated by consumerism and living more and more under cover, whether at home, in the car, in shops or in indoor leisure facilities. Although many popular leisure activities still involve being outdoors, too many young people miss out on free play where they are in control and making their own decisions.

This book aims to redress the balance. It aims to give young people between the ages of eleven and sixteen the impetus to do something they may never have dreamt of doing. Whether you live in the town or the country, it is about the freedom to explore and enjoy wild places as part of everyday life rather than as a special event; to get outside for a real world adventure and to face up to challenges; to pit yourself against the elements and to understand the potential of natural materials. Wild places offer a release and a sanctuary, somewhere to find peace and inner calm, even in the confusing world of a rapidly growing teenager. It has been proved that bushcraft experiences can help teenagers understand where they fit in, giving them a sense of purpose, encouraging them to socialize face to face rather than by wire.

You don't need masses of expensive gear – just some basic equipment and a place to go, whether the bottom of the garden or a distant mountain range. We appreciate that family life can be very hectic, but we wish to encourage people to move getting outdoors up the priority list. Try to make the effort and give the time to it .

The majority of bushcraft books and TV programmes focus on extreme survival, which most of us are happy to simply absorb from the comfort of the sofa. *Go Wild* is about accessible bushcraft, with the emphasis firmly on fun and making it real – young people really can get out there and do this stuff!

This book is the result of all the fun and adventures we have had with our own children, Connie, Dan, Edward, Jake and Hannah, and their friends. As they have grown older we have had to change the emphasis of our outdoor adventures from imaginary games to more challenging and exciting activities. We found that once they tasted bushcraft they were keen to experience more.

When thirteen-year-old Edward went to the woods armed with a billhook to make dens with his mates, we were always immensely relieved to see him safely home. We occasionally wondered if we were being totally irresponsible in allowing him such freedom. In our risk-averse society where everyone seems to be seeking somebody to blame, many parents find it impossible to 'let go'. But is it right to mollycoddle our children and teenagers by keeping an eye on their every move, and not to let them find things out for themselves or learn by

their mistakes? Is it fair to expect them to be able to cope with whatever life throws at them when we haven't allowed them to experience risks and think for themselves while they are growing up? Perhaps the biggest risk young people face is taking no risks at all.

Of course accidents can and do happen, but we believe we need to teach young people how to be prepared, making them aware of what might go wrong and what to do in an emergency. Try doling out freedom in little steps until the vulnerable child becomes a hulking teenager, fully equipped to work things out for him or herself. Reawaken young people's senses by giving them appropriate opportunities to judge risk and use potentially dangerous tools. Let them have freedom, failure, success and responsibility. Let them move nearer to the edge, away from their comfort zone. Let them face life head on and live it deliberately. We believe that by doing so you will be helping them on the road towards becoming well-balanced, informed, free-thinking adults.

We have to admit that it has sometimes been challenging to get our teenagers outdoors; Jake came close to having a glass of water chucked over him to force him out of bed on several occasions! Teenage inertia can be hugely frustrating and tough to break. Keep persevering: unplug them from electronic gadgetry and get their friends involved. For generations teenagers haven't complied with

their parents' wishes, so don't be put off if they ignore your well-meaning ideas: we are quite used to this! Try to avoid resorting to the glass-of-water-in-bed trick – much better to inspire their mates to go on a camping trip, get other adults to come up with ideas for an expedition, or even leave this book lying around so they can get the ideas themselves. Make it a priority and do whatever you have to do to get them outdoors! What will make their memories of the future? The day they sat and watched another film on TV and played a computer game? Or the day they climbed to the top of a mountain or slept out in a natural shelter? Over and over again we have found that once young people are out there they become completely absorbed; they seem to be able to let go and find freedom.

We believe in trying to achieve the right balance between freedom and responsibility, between nature and technology, and that bushcraft offers a way to do so. It also helps young people to gain a respect for all things natural and a sense of responsibility for the world they live in. We need to be tuned into the natural world. We need to know how our actions affect it, how to use it without abusing it, how to enjoy it yet treat it with the respect it deserves. So let's make the next generation urban bushmen, equally comfortable in both natural and technological surroundings. And perhaps by doing so we will not only help them spark a lifelong passion for all wild places but also motivate them to ensure that the world will be left a better place for the future.

SHELTER

SHELTERS FROM NATURAL
MATERIALS

TARPAULIN SHELTERS

THE DIY TENT

TREE HOUSES

IGLOOS AND SNOW SHELTERS

HOW TO GO WILD CAMPING

OTHER WAYS OF WILD CAMPING

CAMPING UNDER A ROOF

SHELTER

In their thirteenth summer Edward and a couple of mates used to load an old bag with tools and snacks and then disappear for hours on end to work on their secret woodland den. Similarly, Jake and Dan made a den with their friends, sometimes rushing off there straight after school to heat up some supper over a fire. Like many young people, our children always dreamt of staying out overnight – so we gave them the chance to do it for real.

We took fifteen boys and girls between the ages of eleven and fifteen to the woods, where bushcraft expert Ben Haydon welcomed us with a crackling fire, a steaming kettle and a mound of pains au chocolal warming on a griddle. As he demonstrated how to build natural shelters, we wondered how the children would survive the night surrounded by branches, leaves and who knew what creepy-crawlies. But to our amazement, everyone slept in their shelters, except Charlie, who got too hot in his made-to-measure leaf hut. Munching bacon and egg rolls around the fire the following morning, they shared tales of their adventures – and they all wanted to know when they could sleep outdoors again. Later we discovered just how much they had appreciated being trusted with tools and fire and being allowed to work things out for themselves. If any of them were a little scared in the middle of the night, they never admitted it.

If your idea of sleeping outdoors is taking everything but the kitchen sink to a campsite with all the facilities from hot showers to restaurants, you may think that camping wild is not for you. But in fact even one night away in the middle of nowhere can be a real adventure. It's well worth trying camping without traditional tents and experiencing the pleasure of sleeping surrounded by the sights, sounds and scents of nature and the joy of waking to the glorious dawn.

SHELTERS FROM NATURAL MATERIALS

It only takes a couple of hours to build a well-insulated and waterproof shelter using nature's ready-made materials; you don't even need a knife.

BUILDING A ONE-PERSON LEAF HUT

This shelter is designed to conserve body heat and will even keep out the rain. The smaller it is, the quicker it warms up.

● Choose a site – ideally a tree with a fork or notch about 1m/39in off the ground. Make sure there are no standing dead trees nearby.

● Prepare the ground by taking a few minutes to clear away sticks and stones. The smoother it is, the better you will sleep.

● Find three long, reasonably straight fallen branches.

● Place the end of the strongest branch into the fork or notch, and the other end on the ground; this is the ridgepole. Our boys wedged their ridgepole between the trunks of two trees growing right beside each other. Place the other two branches on the ground as illustrated; then lie within the frame to check it for size.

● Collect masses of dead sticks and line them up along one side of the frame to make a wall. The closer they are together, the warmer and more waterproof the hut will be, but don't let them extend beyond the top of the ridgepole.

● Do the same on the other side, but leave a gap of at least 50cm/20in near the tree trunk. This will be the entrance.

● On each side of this gap push two forked sticks into the ground. These will support a roof over the entrance, constructed in the same way as the rest of the shelter.

● Cover the whole shelter in fallen leaves, starting at the ground and working upwards. If you have a tarpaulin, use it to carry the leaves to the shelter. The thicker the thatch of leaves, the warmer and drier you will be; aim for at least 30cm/12in deep.

When bedtime came, Charlie had no hesitation at all about squirming inside the leaf shelter, putting his backpack in the entrance to seal himself in to his cosy sweet-scented cocoon. Stuffed with enough dry leaves, this hut will keep you warm even if you have no sleeping mat or bag.

A well-made leaf hut lasts for months, so in order to leave the wood as you found it, dismantle the shelter before you go home.

NATURAL SHELTERS FOR MORE THAN ONE PERSON

Once the kids had seen how to make a leaf hut (see pages 18–19), they split into groups to make shelters large enough for three or four, adapting the building techniques they had learnt. Each shelter was different, designed according to location and whim, and most were covered in a loose stick lattice with a thatch of branches and leaves laid straight on top. Inspired by Bear Grylls, some boys built a fire in a small pit just outside their shelter, to keep them warm and deter insects. Before turning in for the night, they checked it had burnt right down to glowing embers.

MAKING A TEPEE

One half-term break, we found ourselves with a large group of children in need of a focus for the day. We packed up some basic picnic supplies, bushcraft knives and string and set off to make a tepee.

● Find five or six long poles, each about 3–4m/9–12ft long, or cut some lengths of hazel.

● Lay the poles on the ground and tie them together near one end.

● Lift them so that they are vertical, with the tied end at the top.

● Pull the poles outwards to form a tepee shape, with equal gaps between each one. The steeper the angle of the poles, the more easily the tepee will shed the rain. If the ground is soft, push the ends of each pole into the earth to secure them in place.

● These children wove long strips of bendy hazel horizontally between the poles to make a lattice, filling the gaps with leaves and branches. A tepee for sleeping in would need a denser lattice and a thicker layer of thatch, but this one was quick to make and perfect for playing in. A group of slightly older children used it as a wildlife hide one evening, hoping to spot some badgers.

● For a weatherproof tepee, cover the frame with a large semicircular piece of tough waterproof fabric with a diameter equal to twice the length of the poles, and peg it to the ground. Perhaps you could leave a hole at the top as a chimney and light a small fire in a fire pan or a simple stove (see page 46); we haven't tried this yet, but it's a project for another year.

TARPAULIN SHELTERS

Boys dominated our bushcraft expedition with Ben Haydon, but the
three eleven-year-old girls refused to be outdone. They borrowed
Ben's whiteboard to draw a plan, and then with a little help they
made this simple tarpaulin shelter, using a couple of pieces of wood
to support a ridgepole at one end and the branch of a tree at the other.
They tightened the tarp by adding a stick to tension the guy ropes (see
photograph above). A simple tent-like shelter can be made using only
parachute cord or rope and a lightweight tarpaulin (preferably with
eyelets; available from army surplus or camping stores), as shown by
these boys.

MAKING TARPAULIN SHELTERS

● Find two trees about 2.5–3m/8–10ft apart. The ground between them should be bare, level and well drained.

● Secure one end of the cord around a tree at about chest height or lower, using a bowline knot (see page 122).

● Take the cord around the other tree to make the ridge; this needs to be pulled tightly and secured with a hitch knot (see page 123).

● Hang the tarp over the ridge cord, securing the edges by pegging each corner to the ground (for making tent pegs, see page 117). For a more weatherproof shelter, attach the tarpaulin to the ridge cord with knots; prussic loops (see page 124) are effective here. If your tarp has no eyelets, find some small round stones or perhaps acorns and place them in the tarp where you need to attach it to the ridge and then wind some cord around the tarp to hold the stones in place (see photograph above). Make sure the tarp slopes at an angle steep enough to shed the rain.

Try making different tarp shelters, depending on the conditions, the size of your tarp and what natural materials you have available:

● Place the centre fold of the tarp along the ridge with the same amount of fabric on each side.

● Place the edge of the tarp along the ridge, and fix the other edge to the ground to create a lean-to shelter; this is good if there is a prevailing wind.

● Make a lower ridge, and hang about one quarter of the tarp over one side and the rest on the other side. Make sure there is enough fabric to fold over the ground to make a groundsheet. If the shelter is on a slope, make sure the covered side is facing uphill.

● Experiment and see how many different types of shelter you can make, and which one works best for you.

THE DIY TENT

Our families celebrated a summer solstice by camping out.
There wasn't a cloud in the sky, so our DIY tent just had to keep off the
dew. Once the shelter was up and we had installed groundsheets and
sleeping bags, we gathered round the fire on rug-covered straw bales for
a feast of curry and smoked fish, washed down with beer and elderflower
cordial. Children, teenagers and adults sat telling stories and stargazing
late into the night. Under that DIY tent we could smell the damp earth
and hear all the night rustlings, and the following morning we watched
the sun come up, accompanied by the dawn chorus.

What you need:
Camping like this doesn't require expensive gear and gadgets, just a few basic tools and some simple equipment:

- An axe and bushcraft knives
- Large tarpaulin or sheet of plastic
- Rope or paracord
- Groundsheet and/or sleeping mats

MAKING YOUR DIY TENT

- Cut two poles of hazel, about 2m/7ft long. Sharpen one end of each pole.

- Make some tent pegs out of shorter lengths of hazel about 25cm/10in long, sharpening one end and carving a notch in the other.

- Choose a suitable location for your shelter on level ground.

- Push the sharpened end of one of the poles into the ground and hold it in place. Push the other pole into the ground 2–3m/7–10ft from the first one, depending on the size of your tarp.

- Fasten a length of rope between the poles, tension it and tie it securely on to each pole, creating the ridge.

- Attach two guy ropes from each pole to secure them firmly in place.

- Slide the tarp or plastic sheeting over the ridge until there is the same amount of material on each side.

- Attach short guy ropes along the sides of your DIY tent, and secure them in place with pegs.

although I have had a comfortable night strung between a fence post and the car. With built-in flysheet and mosquito net, these hammocks provide an excellent solution to wild camping, immersing you in nature.

On a Greek holiday we strung our hammocks between the enormous gnarled branches of ancient olive trees and lay looking at the moonlight glistening on the sea and the countless stars in the unpolluted night sky, with the scent of wild thyme and the soft sounds of goat bells in the background. If we had stayed in a stifling apartment, we would have missed out on such a special experience – and best of all we could lie there scantily clad but safe in the knowledge that the pesky mosquitoes couldn't reach us. Never string one up close to a fire, as the fabric is flammable.

THE HAMMOCK TENT

The ingeniously designed hammock tent is becoming increasingly popular as a lightweight, convenient, comfortable way to camp; we even know a 71-year-old granny who swears by hers! These hammocks are available from good outdoor suppliers. All you need is two strong trees or posts to hang them from –

TREE HOUSES

I have the most wonderful memories of my tree house high up (or so it seemed at the time) in a majestic cedar tree at the bottom of our garden. My father built it from various odd bits of wood, and we reached it by an easy scramble up the tree or, much more fun, the more challenging climb to the 'back' entrance. It was large enough for several children, and there were windows with shutters and a pulley system for hoisting up picnics. I always dreamt of spending the night there but never actually did. It was a wonderful place, up among the branches, out of the adult gaze . . .

A tree house can be anything from a basic platform to a real house built among the branches. You don't need a large garden or a huge tree: a friend of ours made a simple one in his small town garden, using a tree and additional vertical posts to support a platform, and building a roof over the top. At the other extreme, I have seen photographs of a substantial tree house in France, large enough for a whole family to rent for a holiday.

IGLOOS AND SNOW SHELTERS

Who isn't intrigued by the notion of sleeping in an igloo and not freezing to death? Building a proper igloo or snow shelter takes considerable time and skill, but it's possible to make a simpler version. Try having a go, even if you have no intention of actually sleeping in it.

A SIMPLE IGLOO

We made this simple igloo from snow bricks made by packing wet snow into plastic storage boxes. We tipped the bricks out of the boxes and placed some in a circle; then we set a second layer slightly further in and overlapping the bricks in the first layer. As we added more layers, we packed loose snow into the gaps, making sure each layer was stable before moving on to the next. By the time the igloo was completed everyone's hands were far too cold to enjoy it, but we went back later that night with lanterns and hot chocolate.

If you intend to sleep out in your igloo, dig snow out to make a large hole and then build the igloo around it. Place some snow bricks along a length of wall as a sleeping platform. Cut a hole under the wall for a cold sink and entrance; hot air from your body will rise and be trapped in the dome while cold air falls into the sink. Remember to make some ventilation holes in the walls.

HOW TO GO WILD CAMPING

Camping wild is a wonderful way to experience the natural world, and at its best it makes very little environmental impact. But with increasing numbers of people wanting to escape into the wilderness, it is becoming more and more important to camp unobtrusively and leave no trace (see page 156).

WHY DO YOU NEED SHELTER?

Before you make your shelter, consider the weather forecast and what you need the shelter to do. Does it need to keep you warm or cool? Does it need to keep you dry? Does it need to keep you safe, or keep insects and other creatures away? Even in summer the ground can get cool and damp overnight, so perhaps you need to make a bed to prevent heat loss. Just occasionally you won't need a shelter at all; there's nothing quite like sleeping under the stars on a warm still night.

WHAT SORT OF SHELTER?

Don't plan to sleep in a hammock if there's nothing to tie it to, or to make a leaf shelter if there is no leaf litter. And don't over-complicate things. Shelters should be easy to construct and they must do the job you want them to do, using what's around you or a tent or tarpaulin you have brought with you.

FINDING PLACES TO CAMP

The stark reality is that wild camping is not permitted in many places, particularly in areas such as crowded lowland Britain. Wherever you are, find out about organizations responsible for managing wild spaces, and contact them to find out their policy on camping and shelter building. For example, it's fine to camp wild in remote parts of Scotland, but in England you must ask the landowner's permission, except in some large estates and national parks. Always check first – never make assumptions. Consider offering the landowner some payment and reassure them that you will leave the site as you found it.

Camping is about getting away from it all, sleeping outdoors, experiencing the elements and making do without modern conveniences. A busy, fully equipped campsite seems at odds with this, so seek out smaller, more remote sites with easy access to open spaces and perhaps beaches. Better still, find a campsite with no road access: walking in makes a real adventure and you may be surprised by how little gear you will make do with when you have to carry everything on your back.

LOCATING YOUR SHELTER

Soon after we had pitched our tent one evening, it began to rain, and continued raining all night. Poking our heads out the next morning, we found we were surrounded by water; our tent happened to be on a slightly raised bit of ground, but the rest of the low-lying marshy field was totally flooded. Finding the right spot to camp is the first step to guaranteeing a good night's sleep.

● Choose a discreet campsite with privacy and minimal impact on others and the environment. Try to use an area where people have obviously camped before rather than creating a new site.

● Don't camp too near water (in mountainous country a river may rise as quickly as 5m/15ft in an hour).

● When camping in woodland, avoid standing dead trees, which may fall on a windy night.

● Avoid animal runs and burrows, and possible sources of biting insects, such as marshy ground.

● Make sure you have most protection on the windward side. If you make a fire, do so downwind of your shelter.

● Choose a dry pitch rather than relying on digging drainage ditches to keep your pitch dry. Avoid sites where water may accumulate in heavy rain.

● Always consider what impact you might have on the natural world. Avoid damaging plants.

● A good campsite is found, not made – altering it should be unnecessary.

● If you are in any doubt about what you are doing, go and find out more!

WHEN SHOULD YOU SET UP CAMP?

On an adventure in the Botswana wilderness we began pitching our tents in the fast-fading light, but were interrupted by huge lightning spikes shattering the blackening sky and deafening thunder rolling all around us. We retreated to the safety of our vehicle and watched the most dramatic storm; by the time it was over we were surrounded by darkness and we still had to sort out the camp and cook dinner. The children were anxious and overtired. This was not the way to organize an expedition.

Always allow two to three hours to set up camp; once you have chosen your camping spot, fix up your shelter straightaway so that you know you have somewhere warm and dry when you need it.

SAFETY TIPS

● **Always supervise young people when they are using sharp tools.**

● **For fire safety tips, see page 53.**

● **Stow food (and anything smelly, such as soap or toothpaste) away from your tent or shelter, as it can attract unwelcome visitors. Strung up in a tree away from the camp is best, especially if you are sharing an area with bears.**

OTHER WAYS OF WILD CAMPING

If you don't feel confident about wandering off into the middle of nowhere to camp wild, why not try it out first by joining a trip led by others or by contacting an organization which runs courses? We found the Wilderness Gathering, held on an English farm over a late summer weekend, particularly inspiring: hundreds of people were camping out in the fields, yet there was an atmosphere of quiet calm as everyone sat around their fires, just enjoying being outdoors together. Here are some other ways to try out wild camping.

● Organizations offering camping expeditions in the UK include the Woodcraft Folk and the Duke of Edinburgh's Award; other countries may also have the Scouts and Guides, Forest Schools or the John Muir Trust.

● Some outdoor centres offer opportunities to have a go at bushcraft activities – for example field studies centres.

● It's worth finding out what conservation organizations offer – for example, local wildlife trusts, national parks and in the UK the Woodland Trust, the National Trust and the Forestry Commission.

● Many bushcraft organizations offer adventures for families and young people.

For further details, see page 156.

CAMPING UNDER A ROOF

If you just can't stomach sleeping in a leaf hut or even a tent, perhaps you'll be tempted to try camping under a roof. We have had two winter trips to the Lake District, once staying in a camping barn and another time walking to a remote youth hostel with no vehicular access. Located in the heart of the mountains, such places provide bunk beds and a warm fire. There are various options that allow you to 'get away from it all' even if you don't fancy camping wild or using busy campsites.

Mountain refuges

Several countries have a network of mountain refuges ranging from basic bunkhouses to fully manned huts offering food and supplies. We have walked in Spain's Picos d'Europa (shown in the photograph on the left), where huts are within one day's walk from each other; they are cheap and basic, and provide simple food supplies in season. Other European countries offer similar opportunities, particularly in the Swiss Alps. This is a wonderful way to walk in remote mountain areas without carrying too much luggage.

Camping barns

Often described as 'stone tents', these are redundant farm buildings converted to provide basic dry accommodation. Living and sleeping areas are usually communal, but groups can often book a whole barn. Facilities vary, but as a minimum they offer raised sleeping areas where you can roll out your camping mat, a cooking area where you can use your own stove, lighting, table and seating, a water supply and a toilet.

Mountain bothies

These are stone buildings with slate or corrugated iron roofs in the Highlands of Scotland. Accommodation ranges from extremely basic (sleeping on the floor) to basic (sleeping on platforms), and there are no toilets.

Bunkhouse barns

These are converted farm buildings, better equipped than camping barns. Stoves and cooking facilities are provided, and there are usually separate sleeping areas for males and females, with bunk beds.

Bunkhouses

These are other converted buildings, simply but comfortably furnished; they may be run by hotels, sporting estates or individuals. Showers, drying facilities, cooking facilities and utensils are provided. There are separate sleeping areas for males and females with beds.

Independent hostels

These are privately run hostels; standards vary from hostel to hostel. Most are self-catering but some provide meals.

Youth hostels

The Youth Hostels Association (YHA) still have a few basic hostels tucked away in remote areas of the UK without road access. The YHA is part of a wider network of International Youth Hostels which all come together under the Hostelling International label.

For further details, see page 157.

FIRE

BEING PREPARED

MAKING A GOOD FIRE

FIRE WITHOUT MATCHES

FIRE ESSENTIALS

FIRE

In the wrong hands fire is dangerous, uncontrollable and terrifying; it can obliterate natural habitats, scar landscapes, ruin buildings and destroy lives. But we simply can't ignore the fact that young people are drawn irresistibly to its elemental excitement and ever-changing flames. Fire has a unique capacity to transform even the coldest day into a special moment, bringing people together when outdoors.

Perhaps too there would be fewer accidents if more people learnt about fire and in so doing became more aware of the dangers and how to prevent them. In the UK the Forestry Commission and the Woodland Trust acknowledge that the 'Never light fires' strategy is not always appropriate: they have drawn up risk management guidance and allow fires in specially designated areas.

We believe that more young people should experience the excitement of creating an ember from friction between two pieces of wood, and coaxing that precious ember into a flame. With that knowledge they can enjoy the pleasures of cooking over hot coals, relaxing with friends around the warm glow, sharing stories, gazing into the fire's red heart, and feeling safe and secure despite the surrounding darkness.

If you have the necessary materials, it is not difficult to make fire; but it always needs careful supervision, the right environment and the right conditions.

BEING PREPARED

Hannah and Agnes were determined to try making fire by friction, frantically rubbing pieces of wood together, but if they had generated the longed-for spark it would have died away before their eyes, as they had no tinder prepared. Making fire needs careful planning and preparation: like the girls in the photograph below, allow time to collect the necessary materials before you even start thinking about making a spark, and always be ready to put the fire out in an emergency.

TO MAKE A FIRE, YOU NEED:

Permission

Are you in an area where fires are permitted? Always respect the local regulations and check if you need permission to light a fire. If fires are not allowed, just don't do it – use a camping stove instead.

A means to put the fire out

Before lighting a fire, always plan how you will put it out and make sure water is available near by. To put it out, try to burn all the wood down to ash and then spread out the coals. The embers should soon go out. Sprinkle water over the ashes, watching out for hot steam. Alternatively, continue to spread out any remaining ash until you are quite sure it has all cooled down, and then cover the area with soil.

Time and patience

Don't be tempted to rush: slow down and take it a step at a time. Never wait until late in the day to start your fire – it's not much fun hunting for fuel in the dark.

A source

How will you generate that initial spark? Keep matches in a watertight container and use them sparingly. Try waterproofing the match tips by dipping in candle wax – just scrape the wax off before striking. If you intend to make fire by friction or use a flint and steel (see below), make sure you have all the right materials, and always have matches as a back-up.

A suitable site

● Avoid vegetation that might catch alight, such as shrubs or tree roots, leaf or needle litter or even very peaty soil.

● Don't make fires close to tents, hammocks or other flammable materials.

● Make your fire where you won't cause a nuisance to others.

● Check that you will be able to 'cover your tracks' and leave no trace.

● Choose a sheltered location, but remember that you also need adequate ventilation. If it's windy, build the fire in the lee of a windbreak. Be aware that sparks can be blown a long way.

● Avoid rocks and boulders – it takes decades of weathering to remove soot marks.

Most of the fires illustrated in this book were made on a friend's farm and we returned again and again to use the same fireplace.

Fuel

These girls threw themselves into the task of collecting wood at one of Connie's parties, working together to bring it back to camp and sort it into different sizes. To get a fire going quickly, you need each of the following:

● **Tinder** Very dry, easily flammable material set alight by the tiniest spark. The best way to guarantee dry tinder is to take your own supply in a sealed container. Choose tinder with care: a match will light fine twigs and grasses, but making fire from scratch requires fine fluffy materials with a large surface area, such as the downy seeds of willow trees, reedmace, rosebay willowherb or wild clematis, or bird down, dry moss, dried bracken, wood shavings or perhaps birch bark (which contains a natural oil). Some fungi make good tinder, including the black ball of a fungus known as King Alfred's cake; when very dry it lights easily and then glows, rather like a lump of charcoal. In the absence of natural tinder, use tissue paper, toilet roll, cotton wool or even fluffed-up tampons. Tinder flames are short lived and burn at a low temperature; feed them immediately with kindling.

● **Kindling** Small twigs raise fire from tinder, making the fire large enough to light the main fuel source. Choose the driest twigs you can find; they should snap cleanly, leaving no threads of green wood. Don't collect from the ground unless conditions are very dry. Start with twigs the diameter of matches, and then move on to pencil-thick ones. Or try a feather stick (see below), made by shaving the end of a stick into fine slithers; this is a good way to get a fire going, especially in damp conditions. Like tinder, kindling goes out quickly unless fed with larger fuel.

● **Fuel wood** This keeps the fire going for as long as you need it. Use dry wood initially, but once the fire is established you can use some green wood. Not all types of wood burn in the same way: softwoods (evergreens) burn fast and produce more smoke and less heat, whereas hardwoods (broadleaf trees) are harder to light but produce smouldering coals which burn for longer. As the fire grows, put your largest logs on to it; but don't be tempted to make a fire any bigger than you need for cooking and keeping warm.

Air

Perhaps this seems obvious, but many fires fail because they are smothered by too much of the wrong fuel. A good fire has a chimney effect, with the rising hot air sucking cold air into the base.

King Alfred's cake

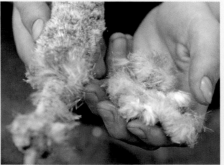

Reedmace seeds

Feather stick

MAKING A GOOD FIRE

Whether you need a fire for warmth, cooking, companionship, keeping insects away or even making smoke signals, make sure it does the right job with the least amount of fuel.

● Clear your chosen place so that you can make your fire on bare earth or, if you wish, lay a platform of green sticks as the base.

● Build a tepee of dry kindling over a bundle of tinder.

● Strike a match as close to the tinder as possible.

● As the kindling starts to burn, add more fuel gradually, starting with the smallest material. Make sure each grade of fuel is burning well before moving on to the next: match lights tinder, tinder lights thin kindling, thin kindling lights thicker kindling, thicker kindling lights sticks, sticks light bigger sticks and these light logs.

● Don't pack fuel too loosely: the flames need to pass from one stick to another or else the fire will burn out in the centre. If you pack it too densely, the air won't be able to circulate.

● If the wood won't burn, blow the fire gently to increase the air supply. Blowing through a non-toxic hollow stem focuses the air nearer the flame.

● The kindling tepee will eventually collapse, but by that stage the fire should be burning well. Either let it form a hot bed of embers for cooking on or build it up again for warmth.

● If you have long logs and no means of chopping them up, feed three of four of them into the blaze to make a star shape; keep pushing them towards the centre as they burn. Only make this type of fire if you have plenty of time to let the logs burn right through.

Safe, low-impact small fires

'White man make big fire, sit far away – black man make small fire, sit close.' The old Aboriginal saying reminds us that you only need a small fire for warmth, cooking and a cheerful glow. This tiny fire was made using just a few twigs and sticks on the bare soil. When it was time to leave, it was easily extinguished and covered, leaving no trace at all.

SAFE, LOW-IMPACT FIRES

How about a fire in the garden?

Fifteen-year-old Jake had invited a crowd of friends round for a party in the garden and felt it would not be complete without a fire. The teenagers lifted turfs and topsoil from an area about 1m/39in square, heaping the turfs together ready for re-laying later and made a fire on bare soil from wood they cleared from the garden. It provided the perfect focus for the evening, somewhere to cook a meal and hang out. After a big fry up the following morning, they dowsed the fire until the ashes were cold. They then mixed and loosened the ashes and soil before replacing the topsoil and turfs and watering them. Although the grass completely recovered after a few weeks, we would only recommend this for rougher areas of garden.

At a bushcraft gathering we saw many small fires being made in a field, but because they were made in a low-impact way, there was no sign of them once all the turfs had been neatly replaced. To improve the recovery of a sward after a fire, make the pit larger than you require and place overturned turfs all around the rim to stop the surrounding grass from being scorched.

Fire in a trench

Digging a trench for your fire limits the area affected and makes it easy to hide afterwards and safer in windy conditions. The walls of the trench reduce the wind and prevent flaring, so you need less fuel. This is perhaps the easiest fire to cook on – just place a grill rack over the trench. Remember to fill the trench in before leaving the site.

Fire boxes, pans and buckets

Restricting fire within a metal container reduces impact. The wide range of options available includes special outdoor fireplaces such as the one shown on the left, and barbecue buckets, being used here for toasting marsh-mallows. There are shallow fire pans on legs or larger rectangular fireboxes with a built in grill. Or why not improvise? Any metal container from a dustbin lid or hubcap to an old wok or frying pan would do. Always raise the pan on rocks, wood or metal legs to avoid scorching the ground beneath. Once the fire has burned itself out, dig the ashes into the soil, or better still take them away with you.

Homemade stove

This wood-burning stove was made from an old gas bottle. It is suitable for use in a tepee and would make a great design technology project.

Kelly kettle

It only takes about three minutes for 1.5 litres/2.5 pints of water to boil in this ultimate of low-impact fires, also known as the volcano kettle. The fire burns up a central chimney, heating water in the surrounding flask. It will work with almost any natural fuel, from bark and sticks to dry grasses and pine cones. We have used a Kelly kettle over and over again to make warm comforting drinks on many expeditions.

Fires on the beach

It is wonderful to sit around a fire on the beach, with the sound of the sea in the background, but always check first to see whether fires are permitted; there may be notices on the beach, but if not, contact the coastguard. Leave as little trace as possible, perhaps by using an improvised fire pan such as this hubcap.

On a sandy beach, dig down a little and make your fire in a hollow; cover it over when you leave. On a stony beach, bear in mind that unevenly heated stones may explode; avoid wet or porous stones – if stones don't sound hollow or crack when banged together they should be fine. Try to avoid leaving black marks on stones; if it does happen, turn them over or bury them.

FIRE WITHOUT MATCHES

We suggest that young people only try this once they have mastered making a good fire using a match. There are many different tools and techniques for fire starting, all of which produce an ember to ignite fine tinder. Making this ember into a fire involves doing the following:

- Before you produce the ember, prepare a tinder nest – perhaps some fluffy material in a bundle of dried grasses (see page 42).

- Once the tinder nest is ignited, lift it in cupped hands and blow softly until a small flame appears. Moving your hands backwards and forwards helps to increase the air flow.

- Place the burning tinder on a stone or piece of bark and continue to blow until it is burning well.

- Now transfer this into a prepared fireplace and gently build a tepee of kindling over it, building up your fire as described on page 44.

FIRE WITH A LENS

The girls at Connie's twelfth birthday party could hardly contain their excitement when they ignited shredded toilet roll using a magnifying glass. This is something so many children try to do, but it's not as easy as it sounds.

● Use any magnifying lens – a magnifying glass, eye glasses (far-sighted prescriptions) or even the bottom of a glass bottle.

● Use the lens to focus the sun's rays on a small area of tinder. A drop of water on the lens may help.

● Keep the lens very still so that the rays stay

on one spot for long enough to set the tinder alight; this is much easier if you rest the lens on a log at the required angle.

● Blow gently on the smoking area to increase the size of the ember.

FIRE WITH A SPARK GENERATOR

This fire stick consists of a steel striker attached by a cord to a rod of pyrophoric alloy 'flint'. Striking them together produces a shower of white-hot sparks. Jake and Ben can now use these to create sparks more quickly than lighting a match; they like to set each other challenges, such as getting a fire started on a wet beach. This is probably the most reliable and practical method of making fire in difficult conditions. Fire sticks are available from good outdoor shops and bushcraft websites – see Further Information on page 156.

● Place a tinder bundle on some dry bark, a stone or perhaps a spade close to your fireplace.

● Hold the flint rod with its tip touching the tinder. With the steel striker in the other hand, strike the flint at an angle while applying consistent speed and pressure. This should produce a shower of sparks. Expect a lot of trial and error and some sore fingers before you produce enough sparks to ignite your tinder – but keep on trying!

FIRE BY FRICTION

All friction methods generate a tiny ember of fine scorched wood dust. Producing enough heat to make the ember isn't easy; is your family up to the challenge? If you manage to produce a little pile of smoking embers, gently tip them into a prepared tinder nest and blow until it catches alight.

The bow drill method

This is wonderfully satisfying when it works, but the co-ordination of motion and pressure required can be pretty tricky. You use a bow to move a drill with speed and consistency to create friction; success is not a demonstration of how fast and furious you work but about care and efficiency. Learn the skill by using an existing bow and drill, and then have a go at making your own set from scratch. This method is much easier if two people work as a team: one applies pressure to the drill and the other works the bow.

Working the bow drill

● Place the fireboard on a piece of dry bark or a stone – this is there to catch the embers. Make sure the tinder is ready, next to the fireboard.

● Twist the bowstring once around the drill, and then place the pointed end of the drill into one of the prepared fireboard notches. Hold the end of the bow and place the pressure plate on top of the drill with the other hand. Press down on the pressure plate while pushing the bow backwards and forwards with a rapid even motion to turn the drill. The resulting friction between the bottom of the drill and the fireboard should create an ember that falls on to the bark or stone beneath.

What you need:

● A 'fireboard' or base plate – a flat piece of softwood. Cut a series of V-shaped notches in the side of the plate.

● A prepared nest of dried grasses lined with tinder, just the right size to hold in your cupped hands.

● A 'drill' made from a piece of strong hardwood and cut to a length of about 38cm/15in. One end should be rounded and the other carved to a point.

● A 'bow' made from a length of strong hardwood. Tie a piece of cord to both ends; this bowstring should be quite slack as it has to wrap around the drill.

● A 'pressure plate' – a small piece of hardwood used to press down on the drill. Carve a notch in the centre, large enough to take the round end of the drill.

The hand drill method

Jake tried making fire using a hand drill, one of the world's oldest and most widespread friction methods. He made a long smooth hazel drill and prepared a notch on a base plate, and then twisted the drill between his hands. Despite great determination he didn't succeed; it is difficult to maintain the friction for long enough. It works best in hot climates with very dry wood.

● Make a long drill as straight and smooth as possible – rough bits can cause blisters.

● Make the base plate or hearth as above, from the same type of wood as the drill, and carve a small notch.

● Place an ember tray beneath the hearth, as above.

● Rotate the drill between your palms with a steady downward pressure, working from top to bottom.

● Spit on your hands to improve your grip and help maintain the friction. Good luck!

The fire plough

When in New Zealand Agnes had made fire by rubbing one dry stick against another along the grain of a piece of wood. To do this, carve a flat surface into the larger stick and then start to move or 'plough' the drill along the grain, creating a groove and gradually increasing your speed. The theory is that this produces tinder and then ignites it, but it is definitely not as easy as it sounds!

FIRE ESSENTIALS

SAFETY TIPS

- Be sure that your party has the skills to make a safe fire.

- Don't make fire near trees or over-exposed roots.

- Make fire on mineral soil. Remove any flammable leaf or needle litter and then replace it before you leave the site.

- Always make a note of the wind's direction and don't light a fire in very windy weather. A strong wind makes fires get out of control or produce sparks. If a wind gets up while your fire is burning, watch the fire and let it die down if need be.

- Never light a fire in excessively dry conditions.

- Keep wood supplies away from your fire.

- Never leave a fire unattended.

- Don't make your fire close to tents, hammocks or other flammable materials.

- Always let your fire burn down to embers before settling down for the night.

- Always supervise children and young people when using fire.

- Have a supply of water near by, in case you need to extinguish the fire or soothe burns.

- Make fire and enjoy it, but never underestimate its power.

Leaving no trace

- Make your fire in a quiet area where you will have privacy and won't disturb others.

- If there is an existing fire ring, use it.

- Insensitive use of fire leaves unpleasant and unsightly after-effects; the next party to visit the site will not want to find old fire rings, blackened rocks or chunks of half-burnt wood.

- Is there a plentiful supply of dry wood? In some environments the regeneration of wood may not keep pace with the demand for firewood. Never denude forests of dead wood, which provides a valuable habitat for many wild creatures.

- Use as little wood as you can and burn it down to ash. On your day of departure, use a small fire for breakfast so all the fuel burns before you leave.

- Scatter unused wood to keep the area looking as natural as possible.

- Take away all campfire litter.

- Do a quick check before you leave – would you want to be the next person visiting the site? If not, tidy up a bit more!

FORAGING

EDIBLE WILD PLANTS

FUNGUS FORAY AND FEAST

COASTAL FORAGING

LINE FISHING

CRAYFISHING

WILD MEAT

FORAGING

Walking in a remote Scottish glen we came across wild raspberries. Gathered as we strolled past, each one was an injection of intense flavour. On another occasion the children and their friends discovered a tree laden with little yellow plums. They gathered the golden fruits into pockets, hoods or anything else that might be used as a bag, and a regular walk had suddenly been transformed into a treasure hunt – providing us with delicious fruit for a crumble when we got home.

Natural places are full of food – berries and mushrooms, leaves and nuts, fish and meat. Our forebears survived from hunting, fishing and gathering plants; knowing where to find food was just a part of life, much as going to the super-market is for us today. But today we buy food far removed from its source and wrapped in layers of plastic. Young people often have little knowledge of indi-vidual ingredients, let alone what is in season or locally grown. We believe that going out to find and cook food gives teenagers a better understanding of the world. Foraging can even have a calming and restorative effect; it is not a macho exercise in exploiting nature's harvest. The successful forager takes only what they need and treats the store with respect.

If you are trying to encourage young people to go outdoors, a few boiled nettle leaves could never compete with the readily available junk food that seems to attract so many teenagers. Unlike survival manuals, we wish to encourage young people and families to gather a few wild foods to enhance ingredients brought from home, combining the fun and challenge of foraging with the sat-isfaction of a decent meal. Allow time and patience; bilberries, for instance, the smallest fruit I have ever seen, lie hidden among the leaves of small bushes in the uplands and gathering enough for a meal takes a long time, but is well worth the effort. Young people today expect to have fast food on tap; help them to slow down the pace and look at food in a new way.

EDIBLE WILD PLANTS

On our expeditions we have tasted various wild plants; we sampled some in passing, made seasonal snacks and used herbs to flavour meals we were cooking over a fire. See what edible plants you can find in your area – get hold of a guide book or look out for organized foraging expeditions (see **Further Information**, page 156).
Here are a few we have tried.

Marjoram

Known as oregano in Mediterranean countries, this is a common summer-flowering herb in chalk country. Gather it just before the flowers open and add to vegetable dishes or serve with tomatoes. We used it here to flavour some bread we cooked over a fire.

Elderberries

The common shrub elder is often laden with berries in the early autumn, providing a feast for the birds. My brother-in-law remembers being given hot elderberry cordial as a child to ward off colds.

Juniper

This evergreen shrub produces small aromatic berries with a purple sheen. Best known as an ingredient of gin, they are also great for flavouring stews.

Nettles

Gather the tips of nettles in the spring and early summer when they are young. Ben and the boys tried cooking them directly over the fire; the process of wilting somehow stops them from stinging your mouth. Nettles are extremely rich in vitamins, and make a very good soup.

Marjoram

Elderberry

Juniper

Nettle

Sweet chestnut

Hazelnuts

Nuts

Rich in protein and fat, these are one of the best survival foods. They are also an important food source for wildlife, so don't be tempted to over-collect. We tried roasting hazelnuts in the embers of the fire for a few minutes, and then shelling them with the aid of the back of an axe. They were so delicious that everyone clamoured to try them.

Wood sorrel

Wood sorrel

Since I've introduced my children to the fresh lemony tang of these pale green heart-shaped leaves they always search for them when out in the woods. They are only to be eaten as a snack, as wood sorrel is slightly toxic in large quantities.

Wild herb teas

For a refreshing and tasty drink, try collecting wild herbs, such as chamomile, fennel or mint, and making tea on the spot. Take a Kelly kettle (see page 47) out with you or a little stove and simply boil up some water and pour it over your wild herbs to make a brew; taste and remove the leaves when the tea is strong enough.

Fennel

Hazelnut

Burdock

On a spring outing we came across the huge leaves of burdock growing at the edge of a field, and a friend recommended eating the roots. We dug some up, peeled them and roasted them in the ashes of a small fire; they were somewhat tough but tasted a little like asparagus. We have since discovered that the roots are best eaten in the autumn, after they have stored up their goodness, but the leaf stems can be collected from May and the leaves in June and July. The roots, stems and leaves of burdock can be eaten raw or boiled – in Japan it is cultivated as a vegetable. To cook burdock roots, clean off the roots then wrap in burdock leaves and roast in hot ashes until soft; serve with soy sauce. To cook burdock stems, use the young shoots, leaf stems and flower stalks, peel to leave the soft core, then boil for up to ten minutes and serve with butter and black pepper.

SAFETY TIPS for plant foraging

● **Always take a field guide. There are several excellent books specifically on gathering and cooking wild foods (see page 157). Note that some tend to focus on identifying flowers or fruit, when it may be the leaves you are most interested in.**

● **Never eat anything you are unsure of – the differences between a poisonous plant and an edible plant can be very subtle. Start with very familiar species such as the nettle or dandelion.**

● **Collect away from roads and other sources of pollution.**

Dos and Don'ts

● Why not go out with an expert? Look out for organized foraging courses in your area.

● Always check on the local laws regarding the collection of wild plants.

● Forage according to this Lakota Sioux proverb: 'Search until you find the plant you want, but don't pick it until you find another cluster of the same plant. Only then can you forage – ensuring no plant becomes extinct through over-harvesting.' Only collect plentiful species and leave enough behind for wild animals and other foragers. Snacking is more sustainable than feasting.

● Avoid damaging or trampling the plants you collect from and others growing near by.

● If straying off a public right of way, ask the landowner for permission to forage.

FUNGUS FORAY AND FEAST

Deep in the forest on a mild October afternoon, Connie and Carolyn searched among the carpet of moss and leaf litter. Every now and again there was a cry – 'Peter, come over here! What's this?' – as they found yet another different toadstool. They were amazed by the variety of shape and colour, from the bright orange stag's horn to the moss-like white coral fungus as well as the more familiar 'mushroom' shapes.

Peter, a friend, was taking us on a fungus foray. Inspired by his enthusiasm, we searched for as many different types as we could find. These strange plants weave their web of microscopic mycelia through rotting vegetation. Autumn's warm, damp weather provides ideal growing conditions for the fruiting bodies, emerging as if by magic to release millions of spores. Try searching on autumn mornings when the fungi are at their freshest. Some last only a few hours but larger species may last four to five days. A few species, notably the bracket fungi, are visible all year round and live for many years. Fungi are present in every type of habitat across the world, and many species are widely distributed in both temperate and tropical countries. With over 12,000 species in the British Isles alone, the variety is overwhelming.

Only a few species are deadly poisonous; several make you feel ill, most of them are just not very tasty – and some are truly delicious. Peter's top tip is to eat only the ones described in the guidebook as either 'very good' or 'excellent'. It isn't only the classic 'mushroom' shapes that are good to eat: the chanterelle, a yellow funnel-shaped fungus, is one of the tastiest of all.

One fungus foray can confuse rather than enlighten, making you very aware of how careful you must be. Hannah found a white fungus; it looked a bit like two puffballs joined together, but Peter told her it was the early stage of growth and might be poisonous. He advised us not to gather anything that was still at the 'button' stage, but to wait until the cap has opened out fully so you can see exactly what you are dealing with. We recommend going on an organized fungus foray with a leader who knows what they are talking about. Expect to use all your senses; on our foray we found species that smelt of almonds and aniseed, and I have smelt one with a distinct scent of crabmeat! We found many boletes or ceps, distinguished by their fat stems, brown caps and yellowy spongy gills. Most boletes bruise blue or black when you touch them, and the more brightly coloured ones should be avoided.

The razor strop fungus fascinated the boys, who had seen it on a survival programme. Also known as the birch bracket, it can be used to carry fire and dried slices of it can be used to sharpen knives. We had some drying on the back of the aga for several weeks, attracting a lot of curiosity from visitors.

Having collected a basket of edible fungi, the children cut them up, commenting on the range of colours and textures. They used a special fungus knife from France, which has a serrated curved blade and a brush for wiping the caps clean. We fried the fungi with butter and garlic in a cast-iron pan over a small fire. As we dished out the multi-coloured mix of mushrooms on slices of bread, I wondered how expert our expert was. But everyone, even Carolyn, who normally avoids mushrooms, enjoyed this delicious fungus feast. Getting involved with gathering and preparing food really can transform fussy eaters into true food connoisseurs.

SAFETY TIPS

● **Never eat a wild mushroom unless you are certain of its identification. If in doubt, leave it out. Many mushrooms are poisonous and some are deadly poisonous.**

This is a tricky subject: differences between species can be subtle, and weather conditions or animal damage may alter appearance and lead to misidentification. If you wish to enjoy a fungus feast, it is best to go out with an expert on an organized fungus foray and just learn about a few species.

● **Buy yourself a good local guidebook to edible fungi, bearing in mind that no guidebook is foolproof. Always make sure your identification checks out in every detail.**

● **Only collect fungi that are fully open.**

● **Don't collect old or decaying fungi.**

● **Try to pick the whole fungus, including the base – this helps with identification.**

● **Always wash hands after handling fungi.**

COASTAL FORAGING

Whether you are seeking plants or shellfish, the coast provides exciting foraging opportunities. Here are just a few examples of tasty wild food that you might find.

SEAWEED

Seaweeds are easy to forage and very often overlooked. They are low in calories but very high in minerals. Try adding them to soups or serve raw as a salad with a dressing made of soy sauce, vinegar and a little sugar. You can also fry seaweed in hot oil until it becomes crisp.

Laver is recognizable by its thin fronds, irregular in shape with purple membranes. It grows on rocks and stones on beaches all over Britain. As with all seaweeds, it needs washing several times in fresh water to remove all sand and contamination before simmering until it is slimy in consistency, rather like overcooked spinach. This can be stored in a jar and refried for breakfast. I have wonderful memories of Welsh holidays, eating rather green slimy laver bread fried up in the pan with eggs and bacon for breakfast. It was an acquired taste, but an unforgettable experience. The Chinese and Japanese dry and toast it and use it to roll around sushi and rice balls.

MARSH SAMPHIRE

We found this succulent annual plant – also known as glasswort – in the salt marshes and mud flats in Norfolk, where it is quite a local delicacy. Harvest in July and August at low tide; cut it with a sharp knife and avoid pulling it up by the roots. Wash thoroughly and steam or boil for 8–10 minutes. It tastes similar to tender young asparagus and is delicious with fish.

SHELLFISH

On our Cornish holidays a favourite activity is collecting shellfish to cook on a grill over the fire. Always collect shellfish from clean stony shores, when the tide is at its lowest.

Mussels are filter feeders; only collect from unpolluted beaches away from human dwellings or where sewage or refuse is pumped into the sea. Always wash through at least two changes of fresh tap water. Only gather mussels more than 3cm/1.5in in length. Immediately before cooking check they are alive by gently prising the shell open slightly: if they open easily or don't close up immediately after you release pressure it is better to assume they are dead and discard. Place them straight on a grill over an open fire or steam or boil them. They are cooked when their shells open; discard any that don't open. Add a little butter and garlic just before eating to add to the flavour.

Place limpets upside-down on a grill over the fire or sit them directly in the hot coals so their shells become the saucepan. They should boil in their own juices for several minutes. Once cooked, use a knife to remove the soft guts on top and eat the muscled foot below – rather tough but very tasty.

The long razor-like shells of razor clams are often found scattered on sandy beaches, but the shellfish itself hides beneath the sand, leaving telltale holes at the lowest tide. Try making a hole and pouring very concentrated salt solution mixed up in an old squeezy bottle down the hole, and then wait a couple of minutes. Sooner or later the shell will emerge. Hold tight on to the end and pull gently, and when it exhausts itself, pull it all the way out.

SAFETY TIPS for coastal foraging

● **Get a good field guide to help with identification.**

● **Avoid polluted waters.**

● **Beware of tides.**

● **When harvesting shellfish, choose the larger shells, about 15cm/6in long, giving the smaller ones a chance to grow.**

● **Never eat shellfish raw. Boil or steam for a few minutes very soon after collecting them. Discard any dead ones.**

LINE FISHING

As a young boy my father spent hours fishing in local streams and canals; he was captivated by the challenge of outwitting the fish, by the wonders of the natural world and by the chance to enhance the family's meagre wartime rations. He has been a passionate fisherman all his life, and believes everybody should learn to fish.

Fishing equipment doesn't have to be elaborate. On a weekend of bushcraft activities we saw a range of simple equipment beautifully crafted from natural materials: hooks made from bone, wood and antler, and line made from a range of natural cordage. By all means have a go at making hooks from a sharp rose thorn or a bent safety pin, but a small amount of money spent on metal hooks, weights and monofilament line is a good investment. A reel isn't essential, but you do need to make or acquire a rod. Most of the remaining tackle can be made

or scrounged; perhaps friends or relatives have long-forgotten tackle boxes or even a fishing rod at the back of the garage. Anything that resembles food in the water will work as bait – worms, shellfish or simple flies you have tied.

Remember that fish are living things to be respected and treated carefully. If you intend to eat your catch, kill it quickly and humanely with a sharp blow to the head; if you don't intend to eat it, remove the hook as carefully as you can and return the fish to the water.

SEA FISHING

On one of our Scottish holidays Edward and his nine-year-old cousin Hamish cycled off to fish from the pier each evening. Equipped with rods, reels and metal spinners (which mimic small fish in the water), they soon perfected the technique of casting the spinners right out into the sea and then slowly winding them in again. I arrived at the pier one evening to find two excited boys holding up a mackerel. Edward tells me that each time you reel in the line you try to convince yourself you feel a fish on the end, but as soon as you really get one you know for sure! Another way to catch mackerel is to trail a fishing line baited with feathers behind a small boat or canoe; if you are lucky enough to hit a shoal, you will get one on every hook. Connie and Dan have enjoyed using a small hand line with a weight and swivel over the side of our boat; any fish they catch is a perfect supplement to our holiday lunch of bread and tomatoes.

We baked the boys' mackerel in the oven, but they are also good grilled or smoked. Mackerel

is a slow-growing fish, taking about seven years to reach 500g/1lb in weight, so only take what you need. They can be caught off the British coast during the summer months, particularly in the early evening.

SIMPLE EQUIPMENT FOR MACKEREL FISHING

What you need:
- Brightly coloured feathers firmly attached to large hooks
- Monofilament line
- Weight and swivel
- Ball of string or a proper hand line

COARSE FISHING

Almost any fresh water is suitable for coarse fishing – rivers, lakes, canals and ponds in both country and town. Although coarse fishermen generally don't fish for the table, much of their catch is edible. We had a go at with a garden cane, a homemade float, a weight and some string.

Making a fishing rod
● Select a straight pole of living wood about 1.5–6m/5–6ft long, or use a garden cane.

● Tie some string or monofilament securely to one end of the 'rod'. The line needs to be only slightly longer than the rod.

Bait
Many coarse fishermen purchase maggots, but earthworms also make good bait – the best ones are found by digging beneath cowpats. Or try mixing water and flour together to make a putty-like paste.

Making a float
● Find a large feather and remove the barbules with a sharp knife. Be careful not to cut the quill.

● Cut halfway across the lower solid section of the quill to leave a length of membrane. Bend this membrane over to make a loop, as shown. Bind tightly with a few loops of thread and secure with a dab of glue or nail varnish.

● Roll a small elastic band on to the other end of the float.

Setting up the rod
Pass monofilament through the rubber band at the top of the float and then the loop at the bottom. Attach a weight to the monofilament beneath the float, and finally the hook and bait. Adjust the depth of your baited hook by pulling more monofilament through the float. Swing the line into the water; the float should stand upright. Sit or lie on the bank so that you are less visible to the fish – they may be a long time coming, so slow down and enjoy your surroundings! If the float moves suddenly, you have a bite.

FLY FISHING

'We'll not catch anything in such coloured high water,' muttered Jack as he and Edward prepared to cast their rods into the rushing River Tay. Thirteen-year-old Jack's experience was soon evident in his casting ability, but Edward's tangled attempts quickly improved after a few words of advice from Jack's dad. Despite the gloomy predictions, a good-sized brown trout was soon caught and the boys started fishing with renewed vigour – they were hooked!

Fly fishing is, in my father's view, 'the ultimate'. It is restricted to fast-running streams and rivers with good water quality; trout favour alkaline waters where insects are plentiful. You need a decent rod and a special line for casting, but other than that it is light on tackle. A fly fisherman has to stalk, hunt and cast accurately: this is a true bushcraft skill. Beginners should get tips from an expert and practice casting in a large open space such as a field where there is nothing to hook except themselves. Here are a few tips:

- The line must flow freely.

- Imagine your rod as a hand on a clock face. When you are casting, it should only move between ten and two, ten being behind you and two in front.

- When back at ten, pause slightly and then move the rod forward sharply, aiming for calmer areas of water. The skilled caster places the fly on exactly the spot he is aiming for.

- Always cast upstream, aiming for water beneath banks or small waterfalls.

- Edward tells me that you need skill to reel in a trout once it is hooked. Play the fish, letting it go when it swims away from you and reeling it in when it turns towards you.

GUTTING FISH

Prepare your fish as soon as possible after catching it. Rinse it in clean water; then, using a sharp knife, cut it down the mid-line of its belly from its gills to its anus. Remove all the internal organs and the red vein running along the spine, and then wash out the cavity thoroughly.

SAFETY TIPS and permissions

● Always be careful near water; don't let younger children fish on their own.

● Always ask permission if you wish to fish; respect closed seasons and land ownership.

● Don't leave any tackle behind – monofilament and hooks will harm birds and other wildlife. Good fishermen leave no trace.

● When sea fishing, watch out for tides and slippery rocks.

● If casting a fly, make sure no one is standing behind you. If the fly gets stuck on a tree trunk across the river and you pull the line hard, be careful because the fly may boomerang back with considerable force. Take care also when casting in high wind.

● Hooks are extremely sharp and have a barb that makes removal from skin difficult. If you get a hook stuck in your skin, seek advice from an adult, preferably a medical professional.

CRAYFISHING

The group of teenagers did not look convinced. How could we possibly expect them to catch anything using a couple of plastic mushroom boxes, a ball of string and a packet of out-of-date bacon? They reluctantly made simple traps, tying lengths of string to the corners of each box and to fix some bacon to the base. They soon discovered that the boxes floated too well, so they added stones and lumps of mud as improvised weights before lowering the traps into deep water.

Before long three boys were swaggering across the field carrying a yellow bucket. 'Has anyone caught anything?' they asked nonchalantly, unable to keep the silly grins off their faces. In the bucket were two signal crayfish, threatening us with their impressive red claws. It transpired that the boys had caught only one crayfish and stolen the other one from the girls' trap! Everyone was impressed that such fearsome-looking creatures lurked in the river and amazed they could be caught so easily; in fact, a bit of bacon tied on to some string will do the trick just as well. Our supper was enhanced by the delicious crayfish, dropped into boiling water and cooked for a few minutes.

Never catch crayfish until you have checked up on local legislation. In the UK, only trap and remove the signal crayfish. This North American impostor spreads disease among our native species and undermines riverbanks with its vigorous burrowing; it is larger than the native white-clawed species, and has distinctive bright red claws.

SAFETY TIPS

● **Always supervise children near water.**

● **Handle crayfish with care – they have very powerful claws.**

WILD MEAT

The boys were playing at being hunter-gatherers for an afternoon. Their delighted faces would have you believe they caught these pigeons themselves, but they had been provided by a friend who shoots. We had laid trails through the woods but instead of finding the usual treats the boys hunted down ingredients for their supper: pigeons, swedes, turnips, mushrooms and corn. We gave each group of boys a heavy-duty cooking pot, and asked them to make their own fires and work out how to prepare the food.

Chopping the vegetables was almost as much of a challenge as preparing the pigeons, but everyone got stuck in to the job. Then they gobbled everything up. Never again would they see meat in the same way. It was no longer just a shrink-wrapped pack from the supermarket. They had seen it as an animal, learnt how to get the best cuts and then cooked it. Something tells me that if we had served up pigeon and turnip stew at home we wouldn't have had many takers!

Not everyone has the stomach for preparing wild meat, but if young people are able to cope there is no reason why they shouldn't have a go, as long as they follow basic hygiene rules – see page 74. We would never advocate trapping or hunting animals for eating, but rabbits and game birds are available from game shops or good butchers, or perhaps you know someone who shoots. Preparing roadkill is another way to give young people a chance to prepare meat directly from an animal.

MEAT FROM ROADKILL

According to British law, if you drive into a wild animal or bird, it is illegal to pick up the victim. But if the car in front kills a wild creature, this meat is yours for the taking, provided you can stop safely. Only collect roadkill if:

● You know the animal died very recently.

● You are on a small quiet road and it is safe to stop, with clear visibility in both directions.

● The animal is intact with no signs of disease or suspicious death. Many rabbits, for instance, suffer from myxomatosis, evident in swollen disfigured eyes and mouth.

Roadkill taints quickly, so gut it as soon as possible.

PREPARING PHEASANT AND PIGEON

Plucking is fiddly and messy; avoid it by extracting the good breast meat as follows:

● Pluck a few breast feathers to expose some skin.

● Pinch up the skin and make an incision.

● Tear the skin open to expose the breasts, keeping your hands free from feathers, which will stick to the meat.

● Cut the flesh just below the breastbone and then lift the breast away from the stomach. Cut through the major wing joints (poultry scissors are best for this).

● Lift out the rib cage and the breast meat and wash well; cut the breast meat off the breastbone.

● Discard the remainder of the carcass.
This will produce a beautiful piece of meat, which you can pan fry as you would a chicken breast or grill over a high heat. Better than chicken nuggets any day!

SAFETY TIPS

● **When preparing meat, make sure all knives and chopping boards are very clean.**

● **Always wash hands thoroughly before and after working with meat.**

SKINNING A RABBIT

This could be compared to taking off a rubber glove. Take care not to perforate the stomach until you have completely removed the skin — you don't want to mix bowel contents with meat.

● Cut off the paws by scoring with a knife and then snapping.

● Pinch up the fir over the stomach and make a nick in the loose skin with a knife. Put your fingers inside the skin and pull sideways.

● Slide your fingers between the skin and the meat, and then pull the skin off backwards.

● Cut the head off. You will now have a skinless, pawless, headless carcass with little resemblance to a rabbit.

● Repeat the pinching over the rib cage as before and then cut a slit in the meat. Using your fingers, tear the muscle wall apart and expose the stomach. The contents should just fall out.

● Clean out the cavity under running water.

● Cut the meat into joints and prepare yourself a rabbit stew.

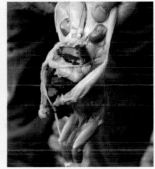

Jake tried tanning a rabbit skin by scraping off all the flesh and fat with a sharp tool, and then washing the skin thoroughly and stretching it out to dry. He had visions of making a pair of rabbit-skin moccasins, but found the whole business rather messy and smelly and never quite got that far. Anyone trying tanning should follow instructions in a book such as *Deerskins into Buckskins: How to Tan with Brains, Soap or Eggs* by Matt Richards.

COOKING
OUTDOORS

THE BASICS

COOKING METHODS

BASIC RECIPES FOR EASY
OUTDOOR MEALS

COOKING OUTDOORS

What does cooking outdoors mean to you? Perhaps it conjures up images of mountains of over-barbecued meat on a warm summer evening, or hardy campers huddled over a small gas stove, boiling precariously balanced pans of bland freeze-dried meals. Imagine instead a welcoming blaze, a pot of bubbling stew and delicious homemade bread baking in the embers. Or some bacon-and-egg butties washed down with hot chocolate while you sit around the fire after a night outdoors.

Cooking over an open fire can be a messy and worrying business, but with a little organization it becomes one of the best outdoor experiences. The secrets to successful outdoor cooking are: keep it simple and make it tasty. Good food is a real morale booster, particularly in difficult conditions.

Whenever we go camping we take along a few spices to liven up our meals. Many young people are suspicious of spicy food, but encouraging them to cook with spices helps them discover how to transform an ordinary meal into something really delicious. The combination of being outdoors, working together and trying things out for themselves encourages children and teenagers to experiment with food – without your having to worry about a messy kitchen afterwards. All that fresh air and activity makes for ravenous hunger and a willingness to try new things; I have even seen a vegetarian girl prepare a pheasant casserole and then tuck in.

If you are unsure about cooking outdoors with young people, have a go in the garden first, where you can resort to a kitchen full of mod cons if need be.

THE BASICS

EQUIPMENT

Don't try surviving in the woods with only a knife, but don't be tempted to take along everything but the kitchen sink. Aim for a happy compromise:

● One large cooking pot and a frying pan, both cast iron

● Kettle

● Wooden spoon and a knife

● Chopping board

● Cutlery, plates, bowls and mugs (make each person responsible for providing their own crockery and cutlery)

● An insulated glove – handy for moving hot pots

● Spade for moving hot coals

● Grill rack

SAFETY TIPS

● **Have the food preparation area a little way from the fire.**

● **Remind everyone about how to use knives and manage fire.**

● **Make sure that everyone knows not to try to pick up hot pans with their bare hands; always have a heatproof glove available.**

● **Don't have too many people cooking around the fire at once.**

● **Have water available for treating burns immediately if need be.**

FOOD SUPPLIES

Stick to a few ingredients, which may be supplemented by wild foods. Your basic larder might contain: self-raising flour, sugar, salt, milk powder, honey, garlic, oil, herbs and spices, stock cubes or powder, tea and hot chocolate. Then perhaps some meat or fish and/or vegetables, along with bacon and eggs for breakfast. And don't forget to take along a few treats as well.

MAKING AN OUTDOOR KITCHEN

Before starting to cook, place everything you need within easy reach, including cooking pots, utensils, food and water. Make sure your fire or stove is ready for cooking on (see page 82). We find it helpful to have a makeshift work surface – perhaps the top of a plastic storage box or a piece of plywood placed on logs.

Work out a cooking timetable, starting with the food that takes longest to cook. Establish basic

hygiene rules: make sure everyone washes their hands before working with food and keep the preparation area as clean as you can. But remember, this is the great outdoors and not a shiny kitchen, so don't be obsessive: just be sensible.

On one occasion several boys insisted on having their own fire and making their own dinner. They loved the freedom of coping with fire, sharp knives, cooking pots and boiling water. The food was barely edible, but they all had a great time and nobody was hurt. Let young people know what the dangers are, suggest ways to minimize risks and from then on let them learn for themselves, even if they fail to produce a decent meal. Next time they will be more organized.

COOKING METHODS

COOKING STRAIGHT ON THE FIRE

For cooking, you need a bed of hot coals; flames just blacken food. Light your fire well ahead of time; it takes a while to build up the hot coals. Make sure you have a supply of dry firewood close by. Having built up your fire, use a log or spade to drag a load of hot coals from the middle to the edge; this bed will become your 'cooker'. Keep the main fire stoked up to create more coals if you need more heat later; you can also increase the temperature of your cooker by fanning it. Make sure your cooking pots are solidly placed on the coals, possibly supported by logs on each side.

USING A POTHOLDER

A potholder allows for more even distribution of heat than cooking directly on the fire. This metal potholder has a chain with which to suspend the pot over the fire; the height of the pot could be varied according to our needs. If you don't have a metal potholder, make one out of three sturdy sticks and a chain or piece of strong cord (see page 119).

MAKING A DUTCH OVEN

We put this cast-iron cooking pot in the heart of the fire and scraped burning wood and ashes all around it to make a Dutch baking oven. The bread we baked was a little burnt on the bottom, but we could have prevented that by placing another smaller pan inside to help spread the heat more evenly. Try using a Dutch oven to bake loaves of bread, vegetables, biscuits or even cakes.

COOKING ON A
METAL GRILL

A sturdily placed grill provides a convenient surface to cook on. Either place the grill over two logs, making sure it is level and stable, or make your fire in a trench and place the grill directly on the ground over the top. Another handy piece of equipment is a double grill with a handle; you can sandwich bacon or sausages inside the grill, which is easily turned over, so you're not likely to lose any supper in the fire.

COOKING ON A STICK
OR A SPIT

Roasting marshmallows on a stick is always popular. To cook bread dough, meat or fish, try using peeled green wood skewers (to make skewers, see page 116). We rolled this bread dough into a sausage shape and wound it round a cooking stick, which we held over hot coals, turning it occasionally to ensure even cooking. This fish and fresh roadkill meat are being cooked in the same way.

A friend told us she has cooked sausages on green sticks pushed into the ground beside the fire and tilted towards the heat. Other than turning them a couple of times, you can just leave the sausages to cook. Alternatively, try constructing a simple spit: bang a forked stick into the ground on each side of the fire, make sure the forks are at the same height and then place a third stick across them. You can either hang a pot from this or peel the 'spit' and thread your food along it for cooking.

SMOKING FISH AND MEAT

Smoking was a widely used means of preserving fish and meat in the days before refrigerators and deep freezes. We made a functional smoker from this biscuit tin. The smoked perch were so delicious that Hannah and Edward wolfed them down as soon as they were ready.

What you need:
- Pliers and screwdriver
- Metal tin
- Wood chips, made from any untreated non-resinous wood: oak, apple, alder, cherry, maple and hickory are particularly good
- Gutted fish
- Wire mesh
- Aluminium foil dish or an old metal container in which to burn methylated spirits or the hot coals of a fire

SAFETY TIPS

- **Use a smoker outdoors or in a shed or garage and take care with burning meths.**

MAKING A SMOKER AND SMOKING FISH

- Using pliers, cut and fold the wire mesh to make a rack to fit inside the tin.

- Pierce a couple of holes in the tin's lid with a screwdriver.

- Place a good layer of wood chips in the bottom of the tin, and place the wire rack over the top.

- Place the gutted fish on the wire mesh and sprinkle with salt and some herbs such as rosemary or sage if you wish. Put the lid on the tin.

- Put the foil dish in the centre of some stones and fill it with methylated spirits or hot coals. An alternative method is to place the tin on the hot coals of a fire.

- Light the meths and then place the tin carefully on top of the stones.

- Leave until the meths burns itself out and the tin has cooled.

- Take the fish out of the smoker, remove the skin and enjoy! Smoked fish is particularly good if mixed with cottage cheese and seasoning to make a pâté.

BASIC RECIPES FOR EASY OUTDOOR MEALS

To Ben, cooking over a fire has become second nature. He conjures up delicious meals from coconut curries to homemade breads, with the help of all the family. Camp cooking needs to be simple and relaxed; don't get too hung up on measuring exact quantities. Have a go at experimenting and having fun. You won't have the control you would have on a cooker at home, so there may be a few disasters! Measure ingredients in any cups and spoons you happen to have available.

BEN HAYDON'S BASIC BREAD MIXTURE

For a savoury version, add salt and perhaps wild herbs, cheese, olives or sun-dried tomatoes just before cooking. If you have a sweet tooth, try adding honey, dried fruit or chocolate chips.

● Take 2 cups of self-raising flour, 1 cup of dried milk powder and up to three-quarters of a cup of water.

● Add water a little at a time to the dry ingredients, mixing steadily to produce a non-sticky, kneadable dough that leaves the sides of the bowl and your fingers clean.

● Knead the dough on a wooden board, until it is elastic and smooth.

● Roll the dough into sausage shapes and then wind it around a peeled green twig (see page 83) and cook over the fire for a few minutes. The dough spiral should slide easily off the stick when it is ready. Alternatively, make your dough into bread rolls and bake in a Dutch oven (see page 82) for about 20 minutes.

ASH CAKES

No pots required – just cook the dough in the ashes of the fire. The party of children looked at us in amazement when we suggested doing this – but it really works. To make the cakes more like bread, add a little yeast and let them rise by the fire before kneading.

● Mix together flour, a little raising agent and a little oil or butter, then slowly add water, mixing all the time until you have a stiff dough. Add a little salt, or if you prefer your cakes sweet try adding a little sugar and some wild berries.

● Knead the dough and then mould it into rounded shapes.

● Place the cakes in the hot ashes where there are no flames. After a short while, dust off the hot ashes and eat your delicious fresh cakes.

POORIS AND CHAPATTIS

Indian breads are easy and great fun to make outdoors, and go well with curry.

● Mix about 2.5 cups of flour with less than a cup of water, adding the water slowly as above; then knead the dough.

● For chapattis, make the dough into small balls and then roll the balls into flat pancake shapes. Cook in a very hot frying pan or griddle with no fat until they are lightly browned on each side.

● For pooris, roll the dough into small walnut-sized balls and squash them together in pairs. Roll them flat, sealing the edges. Deep fry in oil in a cast-iron pot over a very hot fire; they should puff up beautifully.

SAFETY TIPS

● **Be careful when cooking in hot oil.**

● **Make sure the pan is on a sturdy base and gently lower the pooris into the oil rather than dropping them in and splashing hot oil about.**

CURRIES AND STEWS

In a woodland kitchen an all-in-one casserole with fresh ingredients is the most efficient way to cook.

- To make a curry, fry up a few spices (e.g. coriander, cumin, chilli and turmeric), and perhaps an onion, in hot oil.

- Add chunks of meat and/or finely chopped vegetables and fry a little more.

- Add water to cover, and perhaps vegetable stock, and simmer until the meat is cooked and the vegetables are tender.

- Reduce the curry to thicken, season it and taste. To make it really creamy and special, mix in some creamed coconut.

- Eat with pooris, chapattis or hot bread. *Bon appetit!*

Make a stew in the same way, but use herbs instead of spices – look for wild herbs such as marjoram, basil and mint or even wild garlic to add to the pot. And if it's the right time of year and you know what you are looking for, try adding some tasty wild mushrooms or nuts.

AND DON'T FORGET PUDDING!

Marshmallows
These are such an old favourite that we couldn't leave them out. Just thread them on to skewers and hold them over the glowing coals; they should go crispy on the outside while staying wonderfully gooey in the middle. No camping trip is complete without them.

Popcorn
Just toss popcorn into some hot oil in the bottom of your cast-iron pan, stir well and then put the lid on when it starts to pop. Either eat it as it is, or mix it into some caramel sauce. To make the sauce, heat sugar slowly in a small amount of water until it has all dissolved. Bring the syrup slowly to the boil. When it starts to caramelize, mix in a knob of butter to produce a lovely creamy sticky sauce.

Bananas and chocolate
These bananas were wrapped in foil with chunks of chocolate and then baked in the embers of the fire. Yum!

TOOLS & WEAPONS

TOOL SAFETY AND USE

STONE AGE TOOLS

CATAPULTS

NATURAL MISSILE LAUNCHERS

BOWS AND ARROWS

PEASHOOTERS

BLOWPIPES

MAKING YOUR OWN BUSHCRAFT KNIFE

TOOLS & WEAPONS

Given the obvious dangers of tools and weapons, it is understandable to want to discourage young people from using them. However, these activities are not only always popular but provide opportunities for developing new skills and handling risk. We believe young people should know how to use a knife properly so that they will respect the tool and be less likely to hurt themselves in the future. Sometimes the best way to learn is from mistakes – a minor injury will ensure more care is taken next time.

On one occasion several eleven-year-old girls tried preparing a meal to cook over a fire, and we were surprised when most of them struggled to use a knife to peel potatoes or slice carrots. They knew they should cut away from themselves, but were amazed to discover that for some tasks you have more control by cutting towards yourself, using your thumb to steady the knife. Surely the ability to peel a potato or core an apple without cutting yourself is a necessary life skill?

We would therefore like to encourage young people to make a range of primitive and more modern tools and weapons, using natural materials, but always with a healthy respect for potential dangers and for the environment. If young people are allowed to use knives reasonably regularly the novelty and excitement wears off and they should become more sensible.

All the activities in this chapter need careful supervision and cast-iron safety rules. Don't use any of these weapons to hunt animals: only aim at inanimate targets. Be aware that by carrying tools and weapons in public places you may be breaking the law.

TOOL SAFETY AND USE

We went to the woods to make weapons with a group of children and teenagers aged between six and seventeen. The boys' eyes lit up when they saw the bushcraft knives, but they weren't allowed near them until they had listened to Ben Haydon's safety talk, complete with gory details about potential injuries. Soon everyone was whittling sticks, removing bark, shaping wood into catapults and bows – totally focused on the task in hand, and enjoying learning how to use and feel comfortable with knives and other tools.

Tool safety is about knowing how to use tools responsibly, and having an awareness of the potential dangers and how to avoid them. It is also about having the right tools in good condition to do the job in hand. Sharp tools may seem more dangerous, but they work more accurately and with less pressure, so are safer. Whenever using tools or weapons, always stick to the rules and be aware of what might go wrong.

While we provide basic advice here on using tools safely, the reality is that accidents do sometimes happen, and the ultimate responsibility lies with those taking part. Consider the risks, accept them, be responsible for your own actions and always have a first-aid kit to hand in case something goes wrong. For more detailed information about tool safety and use, see *Essential Bushcraft* by Ray Mears.

USING A BUSHCRAFT KNIFE

A good knife is the single most important bushcraft tool. These bushcraft training knives have a long carbon steel blade extending right along their handles. The high-friction rubber handle has an excellent grip, and the sheath can be clipped over a belt.

A knife is a tool, never a toy. Make sure that adults know who has a knife – sometimes a penknife can be slipped in without you realizing. Young people need clear instructions on safety and a clear focus about how and where to use a knife. Adults should anticipate what might go wrong, such as constructive wood carving degenerating into mindless vandalism – on one occasion we were dismayed to find several boys carving their initials on trees. Most important of all, when you are out in the wilds you may be a long way from the nearest hospital, so remember the following tips.

● Always take a first-aid kit with you and ensure someone present knows how to use it.

● Everyone in the party, even those not using knives, should be aware of the potential dangers. Accidents usually happen when people are messing around.

● Before using a knife, make sure there is an imaginary no entry zone all around you. To check you have enough space, stand up with your arms spread out and turn around – you shouldn't be able to touch anyone.

● Adopt an upright kneeling position and cut down towards the ground. Never cut over your lap – the femoral artery runs through the thigh carrying large volumes of blood and if you sever it you will lose a pint of blood a minute.

● Work the blade away from your body, and away from the hand supporting the wood. Never cut towards your hand until you can use of a knife with great control.

● Make sure you cut on to a firm surface such as a steady log.

● If you need to pass a knife to someone else, always do so with the handle pointing towards the other person.

● Always put knives away in their sheaths when not in use; never leave them lying around. Try to choose a sheath that clips on to a belt, so that the knife is always with you.

● At the end of each activity session we always collect knives and put them in a bag together. Young people need to realize that these knives should only be used when participating in bushcraft and not at other times.

● Keep your knife and sheath clean.

● Give knives the respect they deserve: always stick to the rules and only use them in the context of bushcraft activities.

USING AN AXE

● As with knives, check there are no people or obstacles near by. My father nearly killed himself once when he failed to notice a washing line above his head and it caught the axe he was swinging.

● Don't try to cut straight through a log or branch; instead make a V-shaped notch at the point where you wish to cut and then break it. Make small, accurate, focused cuts, not large swings.

● Cut away from yourself at all times.

● Be aware that an axe can bounce back if it hits very hard wood.

USING A FOLDING SAW

This handy tool can be folded away safely when not in use.

● Make sure that the hand holding the wood is a long way away from where you are cutting; then should the saw slip your other hand will be safely out of reach. If you cross your arms before you start to saw, your holding hand is always away from the blade (see photograph).

● Find something firm and steady to rest the wood on when sawing.

● Don't push hard – let the saw do the work for you.

● When closing a folding saw, hold the saw on the outside of the handle so that your hand will not be trapped against the blade.

USING A SPOON OR CROOK KNIFE

This tool with a blade on each side is used to carve out the bowl of a spoon. It can slip very easily, so use with caution (for further details, see page 117).

STONE AGE TOOLS

After a good party the night before, the morning was not what Jake wanted to see. To make things worse, we were dragging him and Edward off to some Stone Age workshop for our book. Edward too was dragging his heels, and grunting as only teenage boys know how. But both boys got completely stuck in and by the end of the day they had a collection of arrowheads and knives to be proud of.

Flint-knapper John Lord and his wife focused on working with flint, a versatile material suitable for making into hammers, knives and arrowheads, not to mention lighting fires. Flint occurs as nodules within chalk deposits; the UK's best flints are found in East Anglia, but other places have suitable flints.

Using rocks and a lump of antler as hammers, John made a hand axe and several small arrowheads from a huge piece of flint. He turned the flint, hitting it apparently randomly, but in time he produced a beautiful symmetrical oval hand axe with multifaceted serrated edges – handy for chopping up mammoths! Making a large axe takes skill and a deep understanding of how flint shears, but smaller weapons and tools can be made quite easily; even a roughly hewn flake with a fine edge is a tool that will cut through hide or carve bone.

SAFETY TIPS

● It is best to work with flint outdoors; if working indoors, always wear a mask. Wear eye goggles when hammering flint. Flint is very sharp; always treat it with the respect it deserves.

ARROWHEADS

The boys became quite absorbed with making sharpened arrowheads, and even took some pieces of flint home. Jake later demonstrated his new skill to some younger children.

● Use smooth elliptically shaped pebbles as hammers – they should fit comfortably in your hand. Sea-sculpted pebbles are perfect.

● Find a good-sized piece of flint and with your pebble hammer chip off shards. The size and shape of the pieces will depend on the angle at which you hit the flint. Experiment by applying pressure from different angles and directions to create different shapes. Select those shards that most resemble arrowheads.

● Place your chosen arrowhead on a piece of tough leather or the back of a sheepskin draped over your knee and, using a piece of antler or a small stone, chip along the edge of the arrowhead to create a serrated edge.

● The arrowheads can be attached to an arrow using a whip knot (see page 123).

FLINT KNIVES

Edward and Jake made knives entirely from natural materials that became prized possessions.

● Make a long narrow flint blade and chip carefully along one side with a stone or a piece of antler to make a serrated edge, as with the arrowhead above.

● Cut a length of hazel about 15cm/6in long and about 2cm/0.75in in diameter. Make an incision in one end by hammering in a shard of flint. Remove the shard and then insert the end of the flint blade.

● Using a sharpened flint, scrape bark from the handle around the blade.

● Make some nettle cord (see page 120) and use this to secure the blade in the handle, using a whip knot (see page 123).

CATAPULTS

Catapults, or slingshots, are extremely powerful and great for firing at targets. We have used them over and over again at parties in the woods.

MAKING THE CATAPULT

● Select a living branch with a Y shape and cut it about 20cm/8in below the fork using a saw or loppers; both sides should be of similar thickness. When cutting green wood in this way, always leave the plant with a tidy stump, cut at an angle so that water will drain off.

● Cut the catapult to the size you wish.

● Remove the bark by scraping a knife away from you along the wood. Make the wood as smooth as you can.

● Carve notches each side at the top of the V, by holding the catapult facing away from you and making several cuts away from you at an angle. Then cut straight down to finish each notch (see photographs below).

● Cut a strip of bicycle inner tube about 60cm/2ft long by 1.5cm/0.5in wide.

● Twist the inner tube around the notches as tightly as you can and secure with a knot.

● Use nuts or possibly small stones as missiles. Only fire them at targets such as tree trunks; **never fire towards people or pets**.

MASAI CATAPULT

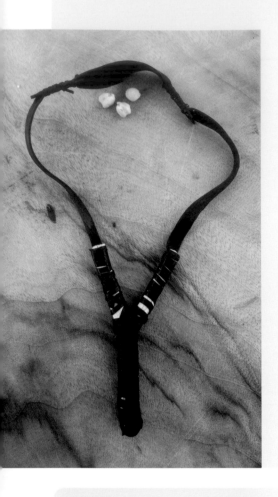

Some friends gave us a genuine Masai catapult. It was small but very powerful, and we discovered that it had been made with lorry or tractor inner tube, which is much thicker than bicycle inner tube. We cut a thin strip of this lengthwise and bound it on to the shaft of a catapult with thinner strips of the same inner tube, producing a catapult with superior firepower. Jake asked me to stress that it's definitely worth hunting in local garages for these stronger inner tubes.

Another design improvement is a pocket for holding the projectile. To make this, either thread a separate pocket along the piece of inner tube or cut one out as part of the sling at the beginning.

SAFETY TIP

● **Never point or fire a catapult at a person if you are going to fire hard ammunition such as a stone.**

CATAPULT PAINTBALLING

Our version of paintballing proved popular with fourteen-year-old boys. As they rampaged through the woods with wild glints in their eyes, we wondered if we would be handing them back to their parents with gaping wounds and missing limbs. But when we gave out knives and delivered a safety talk, everything calmed down; faced with real danger, they listened intently and then set to work making catapults. They were issued with a cloth to use as a facemask and goggles, and asked to camouflage their faces with mud. Then they split into teams to play 'capture the flag', using the catapults to fire flour bombs at each other; anyone hit three times was out! After a pitched battle they wolfed down their picnic and agreed this had been a party to remember.

NATURAL MISSILE LAUNCHERS

How far and fast can youngsters throw a stick or spear? Imagine doubling that distance and speed just by using another piece of wood. This is what the atlatl (pronounced 'atal-atal') can do.

Sometimes called the world's first weapon system, the atlatl uses leverage to throw spears and darts with more power and accuracy than can possibly be achieved by just throwing by hand. This natural missile launcher enabled primitive man to evolve from scavenger to hunter-gatherer, and, unlike the bow and arrow, it can be made from living wood in just a few minutes. Of all the activities in this book this has perhaps been the most popular; it is easy, immediate and startlingly effective. One family would like to see throwing with the atlatl as an Olympic sport!

MAKING AN ATLATL

● Choose a flexible, straight forked branch with a diameter of about 1.5cm/0.5in.

● Cut the branch just below the fork; the main length should be about 50cm/20in, but cut the other side off, leaving a spur of about 2cm/0.75in. The spur has to be at an angle of about forty degrees to the main shaft, and in the same plane; if it points to the left or the right the dart won't fly straight.

● Cut the spur to a point.

This basic design produces a functional atlatl; this could be carved and decorated to produce something a bit more special, like this bird's head.

Since discovering atlatls, Jake and Dan have become expert at making and using them; they started by using hazel but now prefer to use holly, which is a harder wood. They have also discovered that if they can't find a piece of wood with a spur growing in the right plane, splicing two pieces of wood together and binding with tape allows them to make atlatls to their own specification.

The atlatl fires darts or spears; these can be made from coppiced hazel, but any light, flexible wood would do. The spear should be at least as tall as the person throwing it, and about three times longer than the atlatl. Make sure you choose the straightest stem possible; otherwise it will not fly true. Remove the bark, add flights for stability and then carve and fire harden the tip or add a flint tip, as described on page 98.

USING AN ATLATL

● Choose a target – perhaps some balloons hung from a tree or a circle of sticks on the ground.

● Put the spur of the atlatl into the end of the spear, lining them up so that they are in parallel.

● Hold the two together in your throwing hand, as illustrated – put your hand up by your shoulder, and hold the dart in place with forefinger and thumb. It should be in line with your eyes.

● Release it as if throwing a ball: swing it back a little and then throw. At the point of release do a fast hammer-like motion downwards with the atlatl.

It takes practice and skill to become accurate. After hours and hours of practice, Jake and Dan perfected their weapon design and their throwing technique and they can now hit a tin can from a distance of about 35m/100ft.

SAFETY TIPS

Atlatls are incredibly fast and potentially lethal weapons, especially if the spear has a sharpened end or a flint tip.

● **Never point an atlatl at a person or fire an atlatl unless you know exactly where everybody else in the group is.**

● **Make sure everyone present stands well behind those using the atlatls. Wait** until everyone has had their turn before retrieving the spears.

● **Never use atlatls to throw spears at people or animals.**

● **Only use atlatls where there is plenty of open space, as the spears can travel great distances.**

BOWS AND ARROWS

In the quiet of the forest Johnny sat working away with a knife and a length of yew, completely focused on the job in hand. He reappeared some time later with a perfectly curved bow, neatly carved with a thick central section tapering out gradually and symmetrically towards the tips, which had neat notches ready for the bow string. Clearly this was a boy used to working with a knife, but this is something all young people could do, given the right materials and some time to focus.

MAKING THE BOW

● Choose some green wood up to about 1m/39in in length and with a diameter of at least 2.5cm/1in. Make sure it is straight and strong with no knots or twists. We cut lengths of yew (the traditional wood used to make bows in the UK), but oak, birch and hazel are also suitable; try using different woods to see which works best.

● Using the wood's natural curve to your advantage, shape the bow by carving it with a knife to make a thick, strong central section that tapers towards the tips.

● Cut half-moon-shaped notches about 3cm/1–2in from each end on the outside of the curve. Don't make the notches too deep; otherwise the ends of the bow will snap off when you tension the bowstring.

● Select a bowstring of thin nylon rope or paracord (available from army surplus stores), strands of cotton or silk or even natural cordage such as vines (see page 120).

● Attach the string to one end of the bow, wrapping it around the notch a few times before knotting it. Then bend the bow and attach the string to the other notch, using a bowline knot (see page 122). Make sure you can feel tension in the string and bow as you pull the string back even slightly.

MAKING ARROWS

Jake took part in an arrow-making masterclass organized by Wayne Jones of the Forest Knights Bushcraft School. Like so much of bushcraft, arrow making is all about taking your time.

Select a length of readily available hardwood such as hazel
It should be a straight piece about as thick as your little finger and with as few knots as possible. Cut to a length of about 1m/39in.

Strip the outer bark off the arrow
Use the back of a knife. Carefully remove any large knots and smooth the wood, using sandstone or sandpaper.

Make the slot for the bowstring
About 5cm/2in from the thicker end make two small neat notches on opposite sides of the stick. These will be the stop cuts. Turn the stick slightly and make two larger notches about 2.5cm/1in from the same end. Imagine a cross section of your stick as a square – you should now have a notch on each side of the square. Now move the end gently from side to side from one deep notch to the other, slowly breaking more fibres with each movement until you have a crack running to the stop notch. Then turn the arrow into the other plane and continue working it slowly until the end breaks off, producing a neat groove ready for the bowstring.

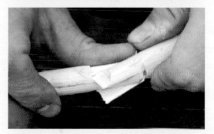

Cut your arrow to the correct length
Stand with one arm out in front of you and the other pulled back with your fingers by your mouth, as if about to fire an arrow. Your unfinished arrow should be a little longer than the distance between your hands.

Straightening
Hold the end of the arrow to your eye and look along it to see where it needs straightening, or roll it across a flat surface to find any kinks. Place any curved sections of the arrow over a small fire and heat the wood to the point where the fibres slide over each other without losing strength. Apply gentle pressure to the warmed sections of the arrow to straighten it. Don't expect perfection; just aim to remove major deformities.

Pointing the end Hold the arrow almost upright over a chopping block with the tip facing down; make several cuts downwards to create a point. Make sure the point is in the centre of the arrow and made with as few cuts as possible.

Fire hardening the tip Place the tip in the fire's embers and gently rotate to drive out moisture. Apply heat evenly around the arrow; otherwise your straightening work will be undone. Take the arrow out of the heat every two minutes or so to check it is hardening but not burning. It should need about five minutes of heating; any longer and it will become brittle.

Adding a stronger tip For a metal tip, hammer an old spoon on a log until it is flat; then rasp the edges with a file. Bend the handle backwards and forwards until it comes off, leaving a small tang. Make a split in the end of the arrow by inserting a knife gently while leaning it on a log. Push the metal into the split and bind tightly with a whip knot (see page 123).

Fletchings These steady the arrow's flight by creating drag. Plastic flights are very effective. Cut three pieces of plastic from an old plastic container, leaving a tang at each end. Tie or tape them on to the back of the arrow, leaving a space for your fingers between the notch and the flight. To make more authentic feather fletchings:

- Select three good-sized feathers, all from a left or a right wing.

- Cut each feather in half by carefully cutting down the length of the indent that runs along the back of the quill.

- Scrape the barbs off from a short length (about 1cm/1/2in) of each end of the quill.

- Tie the half-feather tightly on to the arrow with fine cord.

- Attach the other lengths of feather in the same way, at equal distances around the arrow.

SAFETY TIP

● **Only fire at inanimate targets and make sure no people or animals are within firing range.**

What you need
- Tools: sharp craft knife, junior or standard hacksaw, small pruning saw, sandpaper, pencil
- 2000mm-long oak strip wood 29mm wide by 8mm thick
- 760mm of 25mm-diameter PVC-U plumbing pipe
- Rolls of duct tape and insulation tape
- 1500mm of 20mm-diameter PVC-U plumbing pipe
- Short length of pipe insulation to make a hand grip
- 2m thin paracord or any strong string to make the bowstring
- Soft wood dowelling for making arrows

MAKING A JUNK BOW AND ARROWS

While wandering around at the Wilderness Gathering (see page 33), we met a man carrying this amazing bow made out of plastic pipe and dowelling. A demonstration showed it to be very effective and something we thought budding young archers might like to know about. This is a working bow and not a toy. It is simple and cheap to make and we are grateful to Stephen Munn for providing us with the following instructions:

Making the junk bow
- Cut the strip of wood to a length of 1580mm with a hacksaw. With a pruning saw, cut at an angle into the wood to form a secure notch at both ends.

- Fix the remaining piece of strip wood, cut to 400mm, to the front centre of the longer strip and sand the ends smooth.

- Cut the 25mm-diameter pipe to 760mm long with a hacksaw, and using insulation tape fix it in the middle of wood strip.

- Push the 1500mm long 20mm-diameter pipe through the centre of the larger pipe. Secure it with strips of duct tape.

- Now bind the bow securely with duct tape at the ends and at each of the junctions.

- Cut the pipe insulation up one side and tape it on to the bow so that the top of the grip is on the centre line of the bow.

- Tie the paracord or string on to each notched end, using a bowline knot (see page 122). When it is strung, there should be about 180mm between the middle of the bent bow and the string.

- To make simple arrows, cut the dowelling into lengths measured as indicated on page 105. Carve one end to a point and attach plastic flights (see opposite)

PEASHOOTERS

Generations of children have whittled away at elder sticks to make peashooters, popguns and whistles. Our neighbour's son sanded this peashooter until it was wonderfully smooth. He decorated it with a traditional scrimshaw pattern, but instead of scratching the surface and rubbing ink into the pattern, he used a pyrograph to burn the design into the wood. For shooting, dried peas can be used, or perhaps elderberries to make a blood-coloured mess!

MAKING THE PEASHOOTER

● Select an elder stem with a minimum diameter of 3cm/1in, and cut a piece about 20cm/8in long. The longer the peashooter, the more accurately it will fire; however, shorter ones are much easier to make.

● Look at the end of the stick and you will see the soft pithy core; select another hard twig with the same diameter as this core.

● Sharpen the end of the thinner stick with a bushcraft knife and use it to bore the pith out of the elder stem. This can be done from both ends – the longer the peashooter, the harder this is, as the pith gets compacted in the middle. If doing this at home, try using a kitchen skewer, and adding a little water to soften the pith.

● Peel the bark off the ends of the peashooter, making it more comfortable for firing.

● Personalize your peashooter by decorating the wood. Use a thin permanent pen, or have a go at scratching the surface with a nail, rubbing berry juice or charcoal into the scratches, then sanding the outside clean to leave the pattern.

BLOWPIPES

On holiday in the North Carolina mountains we saw children firing darts through river cane blowpipes made and sold by the Cherokees. These simple effective weapons provided hours of fun.

Ben and Jake have made powerful and accurate blowpipes as long as 1.5m/4–5ft out of plastic pipe from plumbers or builders' merchants. The plastic can be a little sharp on the mouth, so cover the end with a bit of tape. Wooden kebab skewers make excellent darts; fold a small semicircle of thin card into a cone and then tape on to the end of the skewer to make a flight. This must fit snugly into the plastic pipe; if the cone is too small the force of the air won't blow it along, but if it's too big the dart will get stuck.

When using a blowpipe, puff out your cheeks and give a quick sharp blow, forcing the dart out of the pipe at great speed. Aim for a target such as an egg box or some balloons. Great fun! But a blowpipe is a potentially dangerous weapon, so use with care.

SAFETY TIP

● **Never fire blowpipes towards people or animals.**

MAKING YOUR OWN BUSHCRAFT KNIFE

Among my husband's most precious possessions is a much-used knife made when he was a teenager. As soon as he felt our boys were old enough, he helped them to make their own knives, producing something they too will treasure for years to come.

This involves using dangerous tools competently and with accuracy, but it is a great project for adults to work on with the younger generation, or perhaps a challenge for an older teenager. Our boys treasure their knives and have become adept at using them.

Internet research revealed several sites selling hand-forged blades, plus the birch bark, reindeer or moose horn needed to make a handle. These materials aren't all that expensive. A handle could be made from any hardwood or antler horn.

What you need
- Tools: drill with drill bits corresponding to thickness of knife tang, file, needle rasp (half round to get a curve in the handle) or belt sander or sanding drum to attach to drill, 2-part epoxy glue, long clamp and blocks of wood, hacksaw, ball pein hammer (rounded-end hammer), different grades of sandpaper
- Leather, tin or bark to add design to the handle. Tin was supposedly used to prevent witchcraft from entering the blade
- A blade, preferably hand forged
- Birch bark or wood, or horn (see above) for the handle
- Boiled linseed oil cut with turpentine, to polish

MAKING THE KNIFE

● Set out the components for the handle and arrange them in a pattern. It will look pleasing if there is bone at both ends.

● Using a drill, cut a slot or hole in each piece so that it fits snugly on to the blade tang. As the tang is tapered, each hole will be different. To make a slot, drill a series of holes and file out the bits between using a needle rasp.

● Once you have lined up the pieces in order along the tang, remove and glue each in place.

● Line up all the pieces and put the whole knife in the clamp.

● Once the glue has set, using the hacksaw cut the tang off to 1mm above the bone or end plate. Carefully rivet it with a ball pein hammer, spreading the point out to a flat surface at the end.

● Now comes the challenge: gradually shape the handle to fit your hand, as in the photograph. Do this slowly with a rasp, or use a belt sander or sanding drum attached to your electric drill to make it quicker. Do a little at a time and keep checking the grip so as to avoid taking too much off.

● Once you have the right shape, polish with different grades of sandpaper.

● Coat with boiled linseed oil cut with turpentine.

Another project would be to make a sheath for your knife and decorate it with traditional scrimshaw patterns. We ordered ready-made sheaths with a knife-making kit from www.brisa.fi, and the boys decorated them. For further information about making antler knives and sheaths, we recommend the comprehensive guide *Antler Knife* by Ulf Avander.

BUSHCRAFT SKILLS

WOODEN TOOLS AND
IMPLEMENTS

NATURAL CORDAGE

A FEW USEFUL KNOTS

LASHING CORD TO MAKE CAMP
FURNITURE

BUSHCRAFT SKILLS

The woods were strangely silent, given the number of young teenagers sitting around the fire. Only the sound of Ben's soft voice and the thud of his axe broke the stillness, as boys and girls watched him craft a tent peg from a length of hazel and then harden it in the fire. But the minute he finished, they all dashed off, eager to have a go for themselves. Of course you could take everything you need with you when you set off for an overnight stay in the forest, but having a go at making equipment is much more fun.

One year we took a friend's rather troubled eighteen-year-old son on holiday with us. This inner-city boy had little experience of the wilds; we stared at his white linen trousers and diamanté earring and wondered how on earth he would cope. We needn't have worried. Equipped with some wood and a sharp knife, he spent the next five days totally absorbed in making his own knife, fork and spoon. It was the beginning of a new era for him: the quiet, absorbing task of whittling seemed to produce an inner calm, helping him to get things in perspective while learning a new skill and producing something to be proud of.

WOODEN TOOLS AND IMPLEMENTS

There is something immensely satisfying about sitting round the campfire and whittling a stick. Before you begin, feel the wood in your hands – each piece is an individual, with its own texture, shape and grain. For the few tools and implements you need for a camp, green wood is easier to carve and can be hardened in the fire, but if you are carving a keepsake, use previously cut seasoned wood.

What you need

- Sharp bushcraft knife
- Spoon or crock knife
- Large block of wood to cut on
- Axe
- Mallet
- Pieces of wood, preferably without knots

Safety tip

- **These activities should always be carefully supervised; the blades of a crook knife can slip easily.**

SKEWERS

We made skewers from these dogwood twigs with their distinctive purple/red bark. Dogwood, a common shrub in many areas, was frequently used for making skewers; its name may be derived from the word 'dag', used in some places to mean a butcher's skewer. Select strong straight twigs, scrape off the bark and sharpen to a point. Thread bread dough, meat, fish or whatever food you like on the skewer and hold it over the fire to cook (see page 83).

TENT PEGS

- Cut a length of green hazel, about 1–2cm/0.5in thick, and remove the bark, using a knife.

- Cut a series of V-shaped notches about 15–20cm/6–8in from one end, turning the stick as you cut to produce a continuous notch all the way round; eventually the end will break off. A tent peg cut like this won't split when struck with a mallet.

- Place the other end of the peg on a piece of flat wood, and then carve a point by cutting downwards.

- Lay the pointed tips in hot ashes to harden (see page 106).

SPOONS

- Find and cut a piece of wood with a slight curve. Avoid using resinous, scented or very hard wood; sycamore is easy to carve and non-toxic.

- Turn the wood in your hands to feel its shape and grain, and decide where the bowl of the spoon should be.

- Hold your piece of wood on a log as though the bowl was facing away from you. Hitting a mallet on to a knife or axe, cut away the sides of the spoon. Twisting the knife as you hit it will produce a curve. Decide on the size of your spoon and cut off as much wood as you need to.

- Cut off the corners of the bowl.

- Carve out the bowl with a crook knife, using a rocking motion so that it cuts with both blades. Make yourself comfortable by the fire and take your time, slicing away slowly until you create the shape you wish.

- Don't make the wood too thin or else it will break. Smooth away all splinters.

- To add more finish to your rustic spoon, take it home and sand it down. Try wetting it, letting it dry and sanding again; then rub olive oil into it to bring out the grain.

COAL-BURNT CUPS

'Apply burning coals to a chunk of dead wood and then blow on them until they burn a hollow': we liked the sound of this, but weren't convinced it would be as straightforward as it sounded. But Jake and Tiddy made wonderful cups after only about half an hour of blowing.

● Select a chunk of dry non-resinous wood. Dried roots from dead trees are particularly suitable. We used chunks of dead willow.

● Carve a small notch in the middle of one end with a knife and then fill it with a few hot coals from the fire. Holding the coals in place with a twig, blow on them gently until the wood is burning well.

● Continue blowing to make the coals burn right down into the wood; there should be a hot red glow, as in these photographs.

● Every now and then clean out the burnt wood with a knife and then add fresh coals. If you use too many coals, the sides of the cup can get too thin – use water to stop them burning further. Jake found that by using just a few coals at a time he had more control over the process.

● When the cup is deep enough, scoop out the remaining charcoal. Scrape out the cavity with a knife to smooth it, and rinse well in water.

Safety tips

● **Use non-toxic, non-resinous wood. We recommend wearing thermal gloves to reduce the risk of burning your hands. Don't hyperventilate.**

POT HOLDERS

● Lash three sturdy equal-length sticks together at the top and then spread the legs out over the fire. You can hang your kettle or pot or even a griddle from a linked chain or a length of cord attached above the lashing.

● If you just want to make a cup of tea using a small pot or kettle, have a go at making a simple cantilever pot holder out of sticks.

● Another alternative is the pot rod. Find a strong forked stick and push it straight down into the ground near the fire. Place a longer stick in the fork, and push one end into the ground or place heavy rocks over it while the other end will hang above the fire and hold the pot.

WOVEN BOWLS

When we were away on holiday with a friend's son, he made himself this woven bowl to go with his beautifully carved knife and fork. Beginning with a thin slice of wood as a base, he made the sides by attaching thin twigs around the edge with glue. He then wove string through the twigs as if he was weaving a basket. You couldn't use it for eating soup out of, but it was a work of art.

PENNY WHISTLE

Edward made this basic but functional penny whistle by hollowing out a short piece of elder, and then carving a mouthpiece and piercing a hole in the side. A relaxing fireside activity – and the whistle can then be used to accompany a singsong.

NATURAL CORDAGE

Plant fibres were the source of binding materials before the advent of synthetic materials. Some bushcraft experts argue that making cordage is the most important skill in a survival situation: without it you can't build a shelter or make a bow. Use it for tying things up, or make it into natural jewellery like friendship bracelets. Suitable plants include nettles, vines, grasses and honeysuckle.

NETTLE CORD

Jake and Edward made their own nettle cord and used it to secure flint blades into wooden handles. Nettle cord is strong and durable, and in the past has even been used to make clothes. Collect the plants in early summer before the stems get too woody. Storing them for a while and moistening before use improves the fibres' strength. An alternative to twisting the prepared fibres together to make cord is to plait them.

● Wearing gloves to avoid being stung, remove all the leaves.

● Using a fingernail or knife, split each stem lengthways and open it out. Tamp it down to make it flatter and softer.

● Remove the woody pith from inside the stem, leaving the floppy external fibres. To make this easier, bend the stem over your finger to break the pith into smaller sections.

● Fold the length of fibres in two to make a V shape.

● Place the two lengths across your knee near the top of your leg, and hold on to the folded end with one hand. With the other hand roll the two lengths of fibre away from you, so that both lengths twist simultaneously. When you have rolled them as far as you can, let go of the end – it should twist on its own.

● Repeat the process until you almost reach the end of the fibres and then knot the end to secure.

A FEW USEFUL KNOTS

One summer holiday when it was too hot to be energetic, we gave our sons a length of rope and a book on knots, setting them the challenge of tying a bowline with their eyes shut. They soon perfected that and started trying to tie it as quickly as possible. For the rest of the holiday there was always a bit of string in their pockets ready to be whipped out at any opportunity. They learnt other knots and set themselves challenges, such as one-handed knot tying. Knowing some basic knots is useful in many a situation, from making a shelter that won't collapse to slinging a hammock securely from a tree.

THE REEF KNOT

Why?

Perhaps the easiest to master, this knot holds firm under strain but is easy to undo. Follow the 'right over left, left over right' rule or else you will end up with an inferior 'granny knot'.

How?

- Hold one end of cord or rope in each hand. Pass the right-hand cord over the left-hand cord and tuck it up through the loop from below.

- Repeat the process, passing the same cord (now in your left hand) over the other cord and again tucking it up through the loop from below.

- Pull both ends to tighten the knot. Check that the knot looks symmetrical.

THE BOWLINE

Why?

The bowline is a fixed loop at the end of a piece of rope; it won't tighten or slip under strain and is easy to undo even after it has been loaded.

How?

- Take a length of rope. Imagine it has a loose end and a fixed end. Take the loose end in your right hand and make a small loop, with the loose end lying on top of the fixed rope.

- Pass the loose end round or through whatever you want to attach the rope to. Then push it up through the small loop from underneath. Take it behind and round the fixed rope and back down through the loop.

- Pull the loose end and the fixed rope simultaneously to tighten the knot.

HITCHES

Why?

A round turn and two half hitches will attach ropes to posts or trees, taking the strain from any direction and working well under tension. This is the knot for putting up a hammock or tarpaulin shelter or hanging something from a branch. A half hitch is a good way to finish off other knots, making them extra strong.

How?

● Take the loose end of the rope around a post or branch, and then around again.

● Bring the end back round the main rope, and back up through the loop this formed.

● Tighten and repeat the half hitch to make secure.

WHIP KNOT

Why?

This is handy for attaching a spearhead to an arrow, prongs to a spear or a blade to a knife. It must be very tight, so make it under tension.

How?

● Hold your arrowhead with the tang in a slot in the end of the stick or handle.

● Make a loop in the cord and lay it with the loop hanging over the end of the stick and the two loose ends along the stick, as illustrated.

● Now wind the longer end of cord tightly round the stick, the tang and the other length of the cord, binding them all together.

● Continue with neat tight bindings until you almost reach the end of the stick and everything is lashed securely in place.

● Thread the end of the cord through the loop as if threading a needle. Pull back on the trapped end of the cord, which will pull the loop back under the binding. Cut off loose ends.

PRUSSIC LOOP

Why?

This handy sliding loop attaches cord on to a fixed rope; it does not move under tension, but releasing the tension allows it to slide along the fixed rope. It is good for tent guy lines, and we used it on a tarpaulin shelter. It is possible to tie it to a branch to make foot or hand holds for climbing up a tree or a rope.

How?

● Fold your cord in half and pass the fold over the main rope; then pull the ends through the loop.

● Keeping the loop loose, take the ends over again and pull through the loop once more.

● Pull tight, being careful not to overlap the turns around the main rope.

BLOOD KNOT

Why?

This is the fisherman's knot, used for securing a hook on to a line.

How?

● Thread the line through the eye of the fishing hook.

● Wind the loose end of line around the other length of line several times, as illustrated.

● Pull the loose end back through the loop by the eye of the hook and pull on the line with one hand and the hook with the other.

LASHING CORD TO MAKE CAMP FURNITURE

A camp can be made a little more comfortable with a couple of chairs or a seat for the latrine. Being able to lash two or three pieces of wood together is a useful skill for making camp furniture as well as a shelter or raft. The type of lashing illustrated here is shear lashing.

SHEAR LASHING

● Tie the cord tightly on to one piece of wood and make a few turns to anchor it.

● Take the other length of wood and wrap the cord tightly around both lengths of wood to about 3cm/1.5in in depth; keep the tension even and tight, and don't overlap the strands.

● Thread the cord up through the lashing and between the two lengths of wood; wind it around the lashing a few times and then secure with a half hitch (see page 123).

● The pieces of wood can now be pulled apart to make an X shape. This could be used for a variety of purposes – these three lengths of wood were lashed together for a latrine seat.

WATER & KEEPING CLEAN

WATER KNOW-HOW

KEEPING A CLEAN CAMP

WILDERNESS TOILETS

WATER & KEEPING CLEAN

Whether you are out and about for a day or a week, water is a 'must have' on any expedition. Tempting though it is to drink from streams or tumbling waterfalls, even crystal-clear waters may harbour invisible dangers. Always carry a supply of water with you, and take more than you think you need. Look after your supply and use it sparingly – it's easy to gulp water down on a hot day without a thought for what will happen once it's all gone. Think about how far you have left to go and how many other people might also be thirsty.

Most of us take clean water on tap completely for granted; it's always available in seemingly limitless quantities. Surviving on a minimal water supply for a day or two is a stark reminder that this is our most precious resource. If young people know that the only water available is what they have carried with them, perhaps they will appreciate the challenge of finding alternative approaches to cleanliness – such as using a twig toothbrush – and discovering how to manage their supplies so that no one goes thirsty. They can also have a go at harvesting safe drinking water from the environment – one of the most basic wilderness skills.

WATER KNOW-HOW

MAKING WILD WATER SAFE TO DRINK

Always purify wild water by adding purifiers such as iodine or chlorine, using a water purifying kit, or by using this two-stage process:

1. Filtration This removes visible dirt, including suspended solids, invertebrates, plant matter, mud and grit. One method is settling – simply let the contaminants settle out over a few hours and then carefully pour the cleaner water on top into another container. The other method involves straining water through multiple layers of cloth, such as a couple of socks or handkerchiefs or a cloth.

2. Heating The most reliable method for sterilizing water is boiling: if the previously filtered water is clear, boiling should remove harmful organisms. Heat the water to a rolling boil and continue to boil for ten minutes if you are at sea level; at higher altitudes add another minute per each 300m/1000ft in elevation.

Always take time to purify water thoroughly – it's not worth cutting corners.

COLLECTING DRINKING WATER

Try harvesting rainwater, dew or water evaporated from plants; it will always be pure, provided you use clean materials.

Rainwater
Make the most of the rain by collecting it in containers, or rig up a tarpaulin or plastic sheet over a large receptacle so that it runs down into

it. Tie something like a T-shirt over the top of the container to filter out leaves or other debris.

Moisture from dew or fog
Harvest water from the air by condensing dew or fog on to a cool, smooth waterproof surface. Dig a hole and line it with a sheet of plastic; the larger the surface area, the more water you will collect. If enough dew is captured, it will drain to the lowest point in the sheet. Don't lie around in bed the next morning, as the collected dew will quickly evaporate once the sun is up.

Harvesting water from plants
Several bushcraft books suggest tying a plastic bag around a leafy branch, the theory being that evaporation from the leaves condenses in the bag. On a particularly hot Greek holiday, we tried it out, tying one plastic bag on an olive tree and another on a pear tree. In those parched conditions it was hard to believe there could possibly be any water to collect, but to our surprise we found about a cup of water in the bag after a couple of days. Although the water looked brown and unappetizing, it was very drinkable and tasted a little sweet. The pear tree water was voted the more delicious of the two, but didn't taste of pears.

A solar still

This is reputed to be an effective way to produce water on a sunny day even in very dry regions, although we gathered only a few drops from the parched Greek ground. The sweat Dan produced while digging the hole somewhat defeated the object!

● Dig a hole about 50cm/20in deep, with a surface-level diameter of about 90cm/3ft. Increasing the depth improves the productivity.

● Place a bowl in the deepest part of the hole.

● Line the hole with moist vegetation to help the still's performance – essential in dry ground.

● Cover the hole with a large sheet of plastic, pushed down to form an inverted cone. Use stones to secure the edges and place one stone on the plastic directly above the bowl.

● As the sun raises the temperature of the air, soil and vegetation inside the still, the resulting water vapour will condense on the underside of the plastic and run down into the bowl. This water will have been purified by condensation.

In an extreme survival situation, safe drinking water can be produced by condensation from apparently unsuitable sources – including seawater and urine!

MANAGING WATER SUPPLIES

How many of us leave the tap running while cleaning our teeth and peeling vegetables? Camping in the woods with limited water is a real eye opener, revealing just how much we normally use, yet how little we really need. So if you are camping wild with limited clean water, how can you manage your supplies?

● Keep water in clean sealed containers, with drinking water in bottles, and water for washing and cooking in a separate container such as a barrel or a plastic container with a tap.

● Make sure everyone has their own drinking water bottle so that they learn to be responsible for managing their own supply.

● Place your water container near your cooking area for easy and convenient use, perhaps strung up on a frame, as in the photograph below.

● Make the most of opportunities to collect water, putting out as many containers as you can when it rains.

● Drink small quantities of water regularly but never take more than your fair share.

● Treat water with respect – never waste it.

KEEPING A CLEAN CAMP

I remember lugging water supplies half a mile on a childhood sailing holiday. The pain of carrying those heavy containers combined with the worry that there might be nothing to drink if we woke up parched in the middle of the night made us good at conserving water. To this day I can still see the washing-up water – it was the colour and consistency of thin soup, spreading a thin layer of food over plates and cups rather than cleaning them. None of us ever got sick; perhaps living like that for a few weeks each year helped build up our natural immunity.

Many of us live such clean, tidy lives, sloshing anti-bacterial chemicals around liberally, banishing dirt and mud, and not tolerating dust or dirty clothes, but the documented increase in childhood allergies may be due in part to lack of contact with dirt and germs. In our view it's common sense to let children play with soil and get dirty now and then. Bushcraft and camping wild are fun partly because the normal rules don't apply – clothes are worn for more than a day, washing is at best cursory and at worst not at all, and cooking is done in the open. However, here are a few basic tips for keeping your camp organized and maintaining some alternative levels of cleanliness.

WASHING UP

● Wash up away from watercourses, and always put grey water (that is, dirty washing-up water) on the ground, not back in a river or lake.

● Never put detergent in watercourses, as it causes pollution.

● Wash up with as little water as possible. Stick knives and forks into the earth for a few minutes; they will come out pretty clean and only need a rinse. Likewise to clean plates and pans use earth, sand or grass. For more stubborn marks, use a pinch of grit. This is not as odd as it sounds, as limestone grit is the abrasive element in some cleaning materials and toothpaste. Rinse everything with water.

● Best of all, reduce washing up by not making any in the first place. Use sticks as chopsticks or forks, make 'natural plates' from stones or wood and eat with your fingers whenever you can.

RUBBISH

There is nothing worse than arriving in a wilderness area to find it littered with rubbish; even in tidy piles, it's a nuisance and a danger to wild creatures. So always 'pack it in and pack it out'.

● Minimize waste by taking as little packaging and other potential rubbish with you as possible.

● All waste – even biodegradable waste – should be burnt or removed from the site. If you are having a fire, burn all combustible waste right down to ashes.

● Plan meals ahead and try to use all your supplies. Never leave food scraps behind; even if they are buried, they will attract scavengers or perhaps cause disease.

● Make sure you have something to collect your rubbish in. A collapsible garden waste bucket lined with a bin liner works well.

PERSONAL HYGIENE

It is many a boy's dream to go off camping and not worry about such dull things as cleaning teeth and washing. But perhaps the bushcraft way is more fun.

● **Cleaning teeth without a toothbrush** Cut a green twig about 20cm/8in long. Chew one end of the twig to separate the fibres, and then clean teeth thoroughly by rubbing with the stick. Make sure the twig is from a non-toxic plant.

● **No soap?** Use abrasive cold ashes or grit for cleaning grubby hands, then rinse with water. Or if you can find a horse chestnut tree, try crushing some leaves in warm water with your hands – they work like a mild antiseptic soap. Fresh air itself works wonders for freshening you up: take off your outer layers for a while!

● **Rig up a shower** Tie a plastic bucket with holes in the bottom up in a tree. Fill the bucket with water and enjoy a brief but refreshing shower!

KEEPING CLOTHES CLEAN

My washing machine never quite gets rid of stubborn grass stains on the knees of my son's jeans, but hanging them up in bright sunshine never fails to bleach them clean. People often don't realize that the sun has sterilizing properties.

● Air clean your clothing by shaking, airing and sunning for two hours.

● Turn sleeping bags inside out after each use, give them a shake and then hang them up to air.

WILDERNESS TOILETS

The eleven-year-old girls were excited about Connie's camping party; they were quite happy with the idea of sleeping in a shelter, cooking over a fire and being out in the woods all night. But how would they cope without a gleaming flush toilet and sweet-scented soap to wash their hands? When faced, though, with a two-mile hike to the nearest loo, spending the entire weekend with their legs clamped together or going to squat behind a tree, they all set off to find a tree. They soon realized that peeing in the woods is a natural, uncomplicated affair.

Most bushcraft books skirt round or completely avoid this subject, yet knowing how to relieve yourself in a responsible and non-polluting way when in wild places is so important. Some friends arrived at their favourite picnic spot on a beautiful nature reserve to find a pile of poo and a heap of used toilet paper just where they were planning to eat their sandwiches. This horrible experience prompted them to ask us to cover the subject of outdoor toilet habits in this book.

We would like more people to feel it is fine to go to the toilet outdoors if there is nowhere else to go – provided they always do so in a responsible way, remembering at all times to treat the natural world with respect and consider other people.

TOILET TIPS

Caught short when out for the day

If caught short while out for a walk, find a discreet place away from a path – somewhere that won't be chosen as a picnic or camping spot and is at least 60m/200ft away from water. Use a stick to scrape a small hole, making it as deep as you can and keeping the soil and leaves on one side. Once you have done what you have to do, push the soil back into the hole. Try to leave it looking as you found it. Wash your hands, using water from your water bottle. If no water is available, search for some wet moss. If you need to urinate, choose a discreet place away from a path or potential picnic spot, and don't use any paper.

What about toilet paper?

Some popular wilderness areas are littered with trails of toilet paper; the route to Mount Everest Base Camp is nicknamed the 'Kleenex trail'. Surely the wildest and most beautiful places in the world should be free of signs of human presence, not littered with detritus.

Toilet tissue takes years to decompose, especially in cool wet climates, although biodegradable papers are now available from outdoor suppliers. If it's safe to do so, burn the paper. Alternatively use leaves or moss: this is a perfectly clean and reasonable option provided that you don't use poisonous leaves.

Preparing a camp latrine

There was a certain amount of giggling and embarrassment when Ben Haydon told the boys about the latrine at our woodland camp. He had strung a tarpaulin up around a small hole, and the boys' first challenge was to dig a deeper hole – no easy task, thanks to the network of tree roots. This was rather a de-luxe latrine, complete with a loo seat made of logs. Ben's rules about making and using latrines are pretty useful:

● Dig your latrine at least 60m/200ft away from water and some distance from the campfire. It should be far enough away from where you are preparing food that flying insects will not trouble you, but close enough for people to bother using it.

● Make the latrine about three spade depths deep, and leave the soil and a spade next to the hole. If the water table is close to the surface, abandon the hole and dig another one.

● If you have a tarpaulin, hang it round the latrine for privacy using nearby trees or strategically placed wooden poles to support it.

● Hang a plastic box containing a roll of toilet paper and some matches on a branch near your latrine.

● Anyone wishing to 'go' should collect the box and then pull the tarpaulin around the latrine.

● The first person using the latrine should put

some dead grass, leaves or other vegetation into the pit; this will speed up decomposition.

● Perch on the bench and do what you have to do. Place used toilet paper beside the hole and set fire to it. Push any remains into the hole with a stick. Only burn the paper if there is no risk of starting a fire; if in doubt, just drop it into the pit. Try to use as little toilet paper as you can.

● Scrape some soil into the latrine.

● Open the tarpaulin and put the plastic box back in its place.

● Wash your hands. If no water is available, search for some wet moss.

● Don't use the latrine for urinating –

decomposition is more rapid if the pit is kept dry. A small amount of vegetable and fruit waste and ashes can be put into the pit, and will help the decomposition process.

● When you are packing up, replace the remaining soil into the latrine and stamp it down well; have you left no trace?

Toilet can

In some wilderness areas it is impractical or illegal to bury human waste, and all solid, and sometimes liquid, waste has to be removed. This is when everyone needs their own toilet can for solid waste. Line the can with absorbent paper and make sure it has a very well-fitting lid, and take it all home with you. Another option is to carry a length of drainage pipe with screw ends.

KEEPING
SAFE

EQUIPMENT

BUSHCRAFT FIRST AID KIT

NATURAL REMEDIES

KEEPING SAFE

How can young people learn about keeping safe if they are always kept in controlled, sanitized environments doing what they are told and not being taught how to think for themselves? We believe that the best way to prepare young people for life in the real world is to let them encounter and learn from reasonable and acceptable levels of risk; and the natural world is just the place to do that, its many dangers making it exciting and challenging.

Soon after we arrived at a remote camp in the Australian rainforest, the owner said, 'Just get your togs and sandals on, grab an inner tube and head off that way through the bush until you hit the river. Then jump on the tube and float downstream; you can get out when you get to that cabin over there.' As we dragged Edward and his tube out of a rocky waterfall and Hannah disappeared off downstream, unable to stop, I wondered if we had made a huge mistake. What on earth were we doing taking our children down this rushing river deep in the impenetrable rainforest? I thought about all those snakes, spiders and leeches the Australians relished telling visitors about, and wondered if it really was true that crocodiles never ventured this high upriver. How many more waterfalls would we have to negotiate? What dangerous creatures lurked beneath the water? Would we all get back in one piece? But with no paths through the forest we just had to keep on going until the river looped back round to the camp.

Before long we were reunited and lying back in our inner tubes as we floated gently down a calmer stretch of river. We stared in wonder at the towering cathedral-like trees covered in a tangle of creepers and epiphytes. It was an experience we will always remember. Perhaps the most special natural encounters are those where we step outside our normal comfort zone.

EQUIPMENT

Whether you are going for a walk in the woods or a camping trip in the wilderness, when enjoying any activity in the natural world always carry some basic equipment.

It's usually the people who haven't used their common sense or planned their trip who get into trouble. One August morning we set off for a mountain walk; the rain looked set in for the day, so we wrapped up in waterproofs and packed a bag with gloves, hats and spare fleeces along with a flask of sugary tea and a small shelter tent. Although we were following a well-marked route, we took a map and a compass. As we walked higher and higher the mist closed in, the temperature plummeted and we needed all those spare clothes. Then through the swirling mist we spied another family. The daughter, who was wearing smooth-soled moon boots, had slipped and hurt her ankle. Her father was trying in vain to find a mobile phone signal while the rest of the family shivered in lightweight summer clothes. Our shelter tent was up in seconds, cutting out the biting wind and driving rain, and things soon looked up after some warm sweet tea. This was a harsh reminder that mountainous country always deserves respect, but if you are prepared and you know where you are going, the risks are manageable.

It's not only mountains that can be dangerous. A section of one of our favourite Cornish beaches always gets cut off at high tide. On one occasion a father and son scrambled over the rocks in the wrong direction as the tide came racing in. We alerted the coastguard, who came to the rescue, but this could have been avoided if they had learnt about the tide or watched what everyone else on the beach was doing.

PLANNING YOUR ADVENTURE

When deciding what to take with you, consider the following:

● Where are you going?

● How are you getting there?

● What might you do there?

● What might the weather be like? (Remember that the weather can be very changeable, especially in the mountains.)

● Is there any local knowledge you should be aware of, such as tide timetables or weather reports? Talking to the locals may be much more helpful than a guidebook or a survival manual.

● Don't over-estimate your abilities. Having the right kit is not enough – you must be able to use it. But don't undervalue your abilities either; the need to remain calm and not panic is perhaps the most important survival tool of all.

● Are you prepared to rely on yourselves? Mobile phones and global positioning systems (GPS) are useful tools for getting you out of uncomfortable or difficult situations, but if they run out of batteries or fail to get a signal they'll let you down badly when you need them most.

WHAT TO TAKE

There is much confusing and conflicting advice on equipment, but we feel there are a few things you should always carry with you and others you may need depending on the season, terrain and length of expedition. Above all, have your wits about you and use your common sense. Know more and carry less!

A few essentials
- Water – without it adventures can be unpleasant at best and life threatening at worst
- Compass – unlike GPS, a compass needs no batteries
- A good map of the local area
- First-aid kit
- Knife

Other useful equipment
- Fire starter, such as flint and steel with dry tinder (see page 42) and matches in a watertight container

- Extra clothes and waterproofs. Even in hot climates it can get very cold at night. Hats and gloves are particularly important. Remember that children get colder faster than adults, so pack more clothes for them

- Sunhat and high-factor sun cream

- Torch with extra batteries and bulb, and/or candles

- Extra food – always take more food than you think you will need, just in case, including snacks to keep energy levels up

- Lightweight plastic bivi bag

- Sensible footwear, such as walking boots

- Waterproof backpack in which to carry your gear

- A sleeping bag and sleeping mat; the ground can get cold and wet overnight, even if it feels warm when you first lie down

- Tarpaulin and parachute cord (handy tip: put it in a plastic bottle to keep it neat and untangled) so that you can make a shelter

Pack for the best-quality experience; if you have a creature comfort you can't do without, take it along – but remember that you will have to carry it. You don't need masses of gear: only take things you will use or which are vital for an emergency.

BUSHCRAFT FIRST-AID KIT

Always pack your own first-aid kit – know exactly what's in it, and how to use it. You may need to pack different things depending on what you will be doing. Place it in an obvious place in your camp so that everyone knows where it is. And prevention is better than cure: reduce the risk of accidents by taking sensible precautions.

First-aid essentials

- Plasters and dressings
- Antiseptic cream, such as Betadine
- Bandages
- Safety pins
- Tweezers
- Antihistamine cream or tablets
- Sun cream

To reduce the risk of accidents

- Have a well-organized camp with basic safety rules (see page 32).

- Always apply strict safety rules when making fire and using tools.

- Wash hands regularly.

- Avoid sunburn and insect bites by wearing long trousers and long sleeves.

- Make sure everyone in the party is aware of the potential risks and what steps to take to avoid them.

- Try to ensure that children and teenagers know some first-aid basics, such as how to deal with cuts and burns.

A fun way to reinforce the message about the potential dangers of fires, tools and weapons is to practise first-aid techniques. You may never need to use them, but you should be prepared. A volunteer could pretend to have his chopped-off fingers bandaged and arrows removed from his eyes; pressure could be applied to bleeding wounds. And be ready to improvise; we made this stretcher by inserting wooden poles through the body and arms of a zipped-up coat.

NATURAL REMEDIES

Most young people in the UK know that nettles sting and that dock leaves are a natural antidote. Some believe that searching for the right leaf and rubbing the angry red blotches just provides a comforting distraction; however, dock leaves contain chrysophanic acid, known to be effective against various skin conditions, so dock really is nature's own antidote. In North America, poison ivy is a real problem, but jewelweed often grows nearby; its sap neutralizes the oily antigen, reducing or even stopping the rash. Wherever you are, try to find out about local plants that may harm you – and whether there are natural antidotes.

Plants and other natural materials have been important for their soothing and medicinal qualities throughout human history and in all cultures. Remedies were probably first discovered through trial and error, and there may still be hundreds of healing and soothing properties waiting to be revealed in remote plant populations or in other natural materials. Here are a few natural first-aid tips.

NATURE'S FIRST AID

● **Mud** Forgotten to take sun cream with you? Just smear yourself in mud to protect your skin from the most damaging of the sun's rays.

● **Soft dry moss** Placed inside a boot, it helps to prevent rubbing and blisters.

● **Sunlight** This has the power to kill bacteria and reduce fungal infections, so let those sore feet out into the open!

● **Sphagnum moss** My father lived on the Isle of Arran in Scotland for a short while at the start of the Second World War and remembers collecting sphagnum moss as part of the local war effort. This wonderfully absorbent moss with its high iodine content and antiseptic properties was widely used as a wound dressing. It is found in peat bogs.

● **Salt** Nature's bacteria killer. Salt water will help clean minor wounds.

● **Honey** Mixed with a little hot water it soothes colds and sore throats, but it also has antiseptic qualities and can be used to treat minor wounds.

● **Pine needles** For a natural mosquito repellent, crush pine needles in your hands to release the resin and then rub it over your skin. Reapply after one hour.

NATURAL CONCOCTIONS

It was a very wet May morning when we set off with our guide Sarah in search of common plants with which to make lotions, teas and shampoo. Before long everyone had forgotten about the relentless rain, focusing instead on gathering leaves and roots and discovering some of their healing and soothing properties. Many modern medicines are extracted from plants through highly complex processes, but some common species can be used quite simply to soothe bruises, relieve insect bites or settle indigestion. On the following page are a few examples of simple plant preparations made from well-known common plants – a way to make children and teenagers more aware of nature's resources.

Sphagnum moss

Hawthorn

Comfrey

Dock wipes

Sarah suggested using the roots to make a cool soother for insect bites and rashes. Cliffie and Frankie tackled the muddy task of digging up the roots with great enthusiasm!

● Dig up a sizable dock root and wash off the soil.

● Using a sharp knife, peel off the outer layer and cut the root into small pieces.

● Cover with a small amount of hot water and leave to soak for a while.

● Strain the mixture through muslin.

● Keep cool in the fridge and apply to irritated skin with cotton wool.

Alternatively, chop up dock leaves with lemon balm leaves and mix with water; soak for an hour or so then strain and use the water to soothe nettle rashes or insect bites.

Comfrey cream

Comfrey, a perennial herb, grows in damp grassy places across Europe. It has a rather bushy growth, slightly fleshy rough bristly leaves and small hanging bell-shaped white, cream, purple or pink flowers. Its other common names, knitbone and bruisewort, reflect its use as a poultice and ointment for sprains, bruises and abrasions. The thick tap roots exude a slimy juice when cut; if peeled, washed, grated and mixed with a small amount of water they produce a thick gel-like paste which can be used to make a stiff but flexible cast, much like plaster of Paris. If the leaves are boiled in water the resulting mixture refreshes tired feet – or try putting the leaves in your boots on a long walk. We collected comfrey leaves to make a cream to soothe bruises.

● Chop the leaves into small pieces and then mash with a pestle and mortar. Squeeze the mixture through muslin to release the juice.

● Mix the extract with a basic hand and body lotion and put in a labelled bottle.

Dandelion tonic

The dandelion is a tasty, nutritious and useful herb that grows in most of the world's temperate regions. The leaves are rich in vitamins and trace elements and may be added to salads. The juice is the most potent part of the plant for medicinal purposes, and is used to make this tonic for indigestion or to settle the stomach.

● Collect dandelion leaves and wash thoroughly. Bruise them with a rolling pin, and then chop into tiny pieces.

● Wrap a piece of muslin around the chopped leaves and tie it with string to make a tea bag.

● Put the tea bag in a mug and pour boiling water over it. Leave to stand for about five minutes. Add a touch of honey to sweeten if you wish. Remove the bag and allow to cool.

Nettle and mint teas

The stinging nettle grows throughout much of the world. Although cursed for its sting and prolific growth, it can be eaten and used to make cordage (see page 120), and has various medicinal uses. Jake and Edward made this nettle tea, but they turned their noses up at its bitter taste. They might prefer mint tea; made in

the same way, it is delicious. Nettle tea helps to stop diarrhoea and mint tea helps to relieve indigestion and flatulence.

● Harvest leaves any time during the growing season; place in a plastic bag and crush with a rolling pin.

● Place the crushed leaves in a container and pour boiling water over them, or wrap them in muslin to make a tea bag.

I like to pick a sprig of mint leaves and pour boiling water over them for a soothing drink.

FURTHER INFORMATION

FINDING YOUR WAY

LEAVING NO TRACE

DISCOVERING MORE ABOUT
BUSHCRAFT

INDEX

ACKNOWLEDGEMENTS

FINDING YOUR WAY

Could you find your way in the wilderness? Many people are wary of exploring wild places. However, the ability to read a map, understand landscapes and navigate with or without a compass goes a long way towards removing fear of the unknown, opening the door to exciting new environments. This bushcraft skill will help young people feel more at home in wild places.

Here are a few tips to help you find your way.

MAP READING

● **Choose a good local map** It should include rights of way and contour lines. Make sure it is up to date.

● **Understand your map** Familiarize yourself with symbols, perspective and scale. Can you visualize the area? Do you know which way the rivers flow? Do you know the symbols for potentially dangerous features such as cliffs or deep gullies?

● **Interpreting landscape from contour lines** is a useful navigational tool. Check the contour interval of your map; it is usually 5m/15ft but in mountainous areas it may be 10m/30ft.

● **Choose a route** appropriate for the fitness of the group and the weather conditions. The shortest route might not be the easiest or safest; in mountainous areas it may be better to follow contours rather than cross them.

● **Distances on maps can be misleading**. According to Naismith's formula the average walking speed is 5km/3 miles per hour plus 10 minutes for every 100m/300ft climb. Always allow plenty of time, and remember that you'll be walking at the speed of the slowest member of your party.

GETTING YOUR BEARINGS

Visual bearings from a known track Find a feature on each side of the track (for example, buildings, clump of trees, a pond) that are also marked on the map. Draw a line on the map going through both features and the track. When you can see the features line up, you are at exactly the point where the line crosses the track.

Visual bearings from an unknown track or open countryside

Find three features that are marked on your map – maybe a lake, the top of a hill, the edge of a wood, or a row of pylons. Choose one in front of you, one over your left shoulder and one over your right shoulder. Draw the sight lines on the map – you are located within the resulting triangle.

Compass bearings

In poor weather conditions or a featureless landscape, use a base plate compass to show you the way. Try this out before having to rely on it in the middle of nowhere!

● Lay the compass on the map, using the long straight edge to draw a line between A, where you are, and B, where you want to go.

● Hold the compass in this position and turn the dial until the parallel north–south lines on the dial align with the grid lines on the map. This sets the bearing.

● Turn the map until the red north arrow on the compass dial aligns with magnetic north; the arrow at the end of your compass will now point to the bearing you have set.

● Holding the compass level, set off in the direction of your bearing, keeping the north arrow pointing north.

FINDING YOUR WAY WITHOUT A MAP

In the days when there was no such thing as a map, we used natural signposts to find our way – the sun, the stars and the landscape itself.

Using a shadow stick

We all know that the sun rises in the east and sets in the west, and this method assumes that at midday in the northern hemisphere the sun will be in the south.

● Push a straight stick about 1m/39 in long into level ground where it casts a clear shadow. Mark the shadow's tip with a pebble or twig, or draw a line on the ground. This first shadow mark is to the west, no matter where you are.
● Wait for about fifteen to thirty minutes, by which time the shadow tip will have moved a few centimetres; mark its new position.
● Position a stick or draw a straight line through the two marks to obtain an approximate east–west line.
● If you stand with the first mark (west) to your left and the second mark (east) to your right, you will be facing in a northerly direction.
● For a more accurate reading, mark the tip of an early morning shadow and then draw an arc around the stick at the distance of the shadow tip. At midday the shadow will be at its shortest, and in the afternoon it will lengthen. Make a second mark at the point where it touches the arc; a line drawn through both marks will provide a much more accurate east–west line.

Using a watch

An analogue watch set to the correct local time (excluding daylight saving) makes an improvised compass, provided the sun is out. If you are in the northern hemisphere, hold the watch flat and turn it so that the hour hand points towards the sun. South lies halfway between the hour hand and the figure 12. Use a blade of grass or a straight twig to mark the north–south line. In the southern hemisphere, hold the watch face with the figure 12 towards the sun; to find north bisect the angle between the hour hand and the figure 12.

Natural direction indicators

Out in the wilderness with no map, no compass and no sunshine? Train yourself to look for natural signs to help you find your way:

● **Landmarks on your way in** Look for landmarks to watch out for on your return – or leave natural markers as a trail.
● **Lie of the land** Get to a high point with a panoramic view so that you can place yourself – use your common sense! Take some binoculars with you.
● **Water** On a wet walk in the Lake District, Jo's family followed a stream down the mountain; it was wet and slippery, but everyone loved the challenge of scrambling down over the rocks to find their way home.
● **Wind** Strong winds can affect plant growth. If you know the direction of the prevailing wind, use this to your advantage.
● **Plants** In the northern hemisphere the most abundant growth of flowering plants, mosses and lichens is usually on the southern aspect, and sometimes the sun's rays may even bleach the southerly side of tree trunks or rocks. But local climatic factors also play their part – so consider such factors as how sheltered or damp a place is; and never rely entirely on one natural means of direction finding.
● **Buildings** If you can see any churches, remember they always face east.

LEAVING NO TRACE

All bushcraft activities should be carried out with
the utmost respect for the integrity of wild places
and the natural world. Go Wild with minimal impact
by following these 'Leave no Trace' principles:

- Plan ahead and prepare.
- Travel and camp on durable surfaces.
- Dispose of waste properly.
- Leave what you find.
- Minimize campfire impacts.
- Respect all wildlife.
- Be considerate of other users.
- Take responsibility for your own actions.

For further information about leaving no trace, see www.lnt.org

DISCOVERING MORE ABOUT BUSHCRAFT

For more information on outdoor
activities and our books *Go Wild*
and *Nature's Playground*, see

www.goingwild.net

GENERAL BUSHCRAFT AND OUTDOOR EDUCATION

Elpel, Thomas J., *Primitive Living,
Self-sufficiency and Survival Skills*, Lyons Press,
2004

Grylls, Bear, *Born Survivor*,
4 Books, 2007

Louv, Richard, *Last Child in the Woods*,
Algonquin Books, 2006

McManners, Hugh, *Outdoor Survival Guide*,
Dorling Kindersley, 2007

Mears, Ray, *Essential Bushcraft*,
Hodder and Stoughton, 2003

Wiseman, John, SAS Survival Guide,
Collins Gem, 2004

The Bushcraft Magazine, published quarterly;
see www.bushcraft-magazine.co.uk

The Wilderness Gathering is the UK's annual
bushcraft festival: see
www.wildernessgathering.co.uk

For information about a range of outdoor
activities and games, see
www.scoutingresources.org.uk

For information on the Forest Education Initiative, see www.foresteducation.org

For details of bushcraft courses and some supply equipment, see:
www.islaybirding.co.uk
www.backwoodsurvival.co.uk
www.wholeland.org.uk
www.woodlandsurvivalcrafts.com
www.wildwise.co.uk
www.dryadbushcraft.co.uk
www.woodsmoke.uk.com
www.raymears.com

SHELTER

For information on good countryside campsites in the UK, see www.coolcamping.co.uk

For information on camping barns, see www.lakelandcampingbarns.co.uk

For further details on mountain bothies, www.mountainbothies.org.uk

For details of hammock tents, www.hennessy-hammock.co.uk

FORAGING AND FOOD

Grieve, Guy, and Thomasina Miers, *The Wild Gourmets*, Bloomsbury, 2007

Mabey, Richard, *Food for Free*, Collins Gem, 2004

—*Flora Britannica*, Sinclair-Stevenson, 1996

Mears, Ray, *Wild Food*, Hodder and Stoughton, 2007

Phillips, Roger, *Wild Food*, Macmillan, 1983

—*Mushrooms*, Macmillan, 2006

Richards, Matt, *Deerskins into Buckskins,* Blackcountry Publishing, 2004

— *How to Tan with Brains, Soap or Eggs*, Partners Publishing, 1998

Whieldon, Tony, *The Complete Guide to Fishing Skills*, Cassell, 2002

For information about foraging courses, see www.wildmanwildfood.com

Crayfish trapping advice packs are available from the National Fisheries Laboratory (01480 483968); for more information, see www.environment-agency.gov.uk

TOOLS AND WEAPONS

Lord, John, *The Nature and Subsequent Uses of Flint*, John Lord, 1993

Avander, Ulf, *Antler Knife*, Ulf Avander, 2004

For information on various bushcraft courses including bow and arrow making, see www.forestknights.co.uk

For more details about the design and materials of the junk bow on page 107, contact Stephen.munn@grapefruitopia.com

WATER AND KEEPING CLEAN

Meyer, Kathleen, *How to Shit in the Woods*, Ten Speed Press, 1994

KEEPING SAFE

Wilderness First Aid Ltd offers courses on dealing with wilderness first-aid and emergencies: see www.wildernessfirstaid.co.uk

INDEX

atlatl 101-103
arrow 104-107, 157
ash 41, 45, 53, 82
axe 25, 59, 96, 97, 116, 117

bacon 17, 72, 79, 81
banana 89
bait 68
bilberries 57
birch bracket fungus 62
blowpipe 109
boletes 62
bow drill 51
bow 94, 104, 107
bread
  ash cakes 86
  basic bread mix 86
  chapattis 88
  dough 9, 83, 86, 116
  pooris 88
bunkhouse barn 35
burdock 60

camp furniture 125
camping barn 34, 35
campsite 17, 30, 32
Capture the flag 100
carving 25, 95, 108, 116, 117, 118
catapult 94, 99-100
  Masai 100
  paintballing 100
ceps 62
chanterelle 62
coal burnt cups 112-113, 118
compass bearings 154
comfrey bruise cream 150
cooking outdoors 76-85
cordage 66, 104, 120
crayfishing 72
curry 85, 89

dandelion tonic 151
dart 101, 109
DIY tent 24-25
dock
  leaves 148
  wipes 150
Dutch oven 82

earthworms 68
eggs 17, 79, 81
elder 108
elderberries 58
equipment 66, 80, 144-146

feather stick 42
fennel 59

fishing 66-71
  coarse 68
  fly 70
  sea 67
finding your way 155
fire 36-53
fire by friction 50-52
fire safety 53
fire stick 49
first aid kit 94, 95, 147
fletchings 106
flint
  arrowhead 98, 102, 106
  knapping 97
  knife 98
flint and steel 9, 49
float (fishing) 68
flour bombs 100
folding saw 95, 96
food supplies 81
foraging 54-75
fuel wood 42
fungi 42, 61-63

grill 46, 83
groundsheet 23, 24, 25
gutting fish 71
guy rope 25

hammock 9, 26, 30, 41, 53, 121, 123
hand drill 52
hazel
  nuts 59
  wood 21, 25, 52, 98, 102, 104, 105, 117
  honey 81, 86, 149

igloo 28-29

juniper 58
junk bow 107

keeping safe 140-151
Kelly kettle 47, 59
kindling 42, 44
King Alfred's cake 42
knife 62, 80, 93, 104, 105, 116, 146
  bushcraft 94, 95, 110, 116
  crook 96, 116, 117
  flint 98
  making 110-111
  safety 94-95
knots 121-124
  blood 124
  bowline 23, 104, 121, 122
  hitch 23, 123, 125
  prussic loop 23, 124
  reef 22
  whip 98, 106, 123

lashing 125
latrine 9, 138–139
laverbread 64
leaf hut 14, 17, 18, 20
Leave no trace 30, 41, 53, 71, 156
Limpets 65

mackerel 67
maggots 68
magnifying lens 49
mallet 116,117
map 145, 146
map reading 154
marjoram 58
marsh samphire 64
marshmallows 89
matches 41, 138, 146
mint tea 151
moss 42, 61, 138, 139, 149, 155
mountain bothy 35
mountain refuge 35
mud 72, 100, 130, 149
mussels 65

natural cordage 66, 104, 120
natural remedies 148–151
natural missile launchers 101–103
nettle 58
    cord 120
    tea 151
nuts 59, 89

outdoor kitchen 81

parachute cord 22, 23, 146
peashooter 108
penny whistle 119
pheasant 74
pigeon 73, 74
pine needles 149
plums 57
poison ivy 148
popcorn 89
pot holder 82, 119
protractor compass 146, 154

rabbit 73,74
    skinning 75
raspberries 57
razor clams 65
razor strop fungus 62
recipes 85–89
reedmace seeds 42
roadkill meat 73, 74, 83
rubbish 136

safety 53, 94, 140-148
salt 81, 84, 149

samphire 64
seaweed 64
shadow stick 155
shellfish 65
shelter 9, 13, 14–34, 123, 125
shower 136
skewers 83, 109, 116
skinning a rabbit 75
sleeping bag 24, 136, 146
smoking fish 84
snow shelter 28–29
solar still 132
spade 49, 80, 138
spark generator 49
spear 101, 102, 123
spoons 9, 96, 117
stew 89
stone age tools 97–98
stretcher 147
sweet chestnut 59

tarpaulin 22, 123, 130, 146
tent 9, 17, 24, 25, 26, 32, 34, 41, 53, 124, 145
tent peg 9, 25, 117
tepee 21, 46
tinder 40, 42, 146
toadstool 61
toilet
    can 139
    paper 138
    tips 138
tools 90–111
    safety 94
torch 146
tree house 26-27
trout 70–71
twig toothbrush 128, 129, 136

volcano kettle 47

washing up 134
water 129-133, 146
    collecting 130–132
    drinking 129, 130
    purifying 130
    supplies 133
weapons 90–111
whittling 9, 94, 115, 116
wild meat 73-75
Wilderness gathering 33
wilderness toilets 137–139
wood sorrel 59
wooden tools 116-119
woven bowls 119

yew 104
youth hostel 35

ACKNOWLEDGEMENTS

The ideas and information for this book come from many sources: thanks to everyone who has shared ideas and provided practical advice and support. Please notify the publisher if there are inadvertent omissions in these acknowledgements, which will be rectified in future editions.

We would like to thank the following people for their help and advice: Peter Creed; John and Val Lord; Robin Hull; Jane and Bob White; Stephen Munn, Wayne Jones (the Forest Knights Bushcraft School), Jeremy Hastings (Islay Birding), Sarah Robertshaw and Dave Watson (Woodland Survival Crafts) and everyone else who shared ideas at the 2007 Wilderness Gathering; Sarah Lloyd and Kate Castleden (Oxford Botanic Garden and Arboretum); Diana Bailey; Heather Francis; Zilpah Hoffman; Chris Langton and David Dunbar; Helen and James Jackson; and the many families and friends who have supported us in so many ways.

We are particularly grateful to Ben Haydon, who encourages and assists the informal handing down of indigenous bushcraft and survival skills through working with groups of families and young people. Email Ben at ben@haydon.org.uk.

A big thank you to all the young people who took part in bushcraft activities: Jack D; Tom U; Jo B; Jonathon and Jessie A; Tristan S; Lily, Charlie and Toby R; Agnes K; Carolyn S; Clifford, Frankie and Anya C; Anna, Tim, Nicholas and Ella V; Jessie, Alice and Johnnie F; Tilly S; Tiggy W; Lucas R; Georgia E; Rebecca and Edward W; Gabriel and Ri G; Harry G; Alexander B; Matt, Tris and Will E; Sam B; Arthur K; Harry T; Anatol S; Olly P; Jack M; Natasha H; Anna, Laura and Ben W; Tallula, Noah and Poppy C; Sophie T; Isabella G; Catherine F; Milly B; Tilly G; Rebecca M; Lydia, Helena and Lucian S; David C.; Luke B; Tsering L; Ella W; Imogen B; Hannah M; Kate W; Ellen B; Jess R; and Sarah P.

Many thanks are also due to our husbands, Ben and Peter, and our children, Jake, Dan, Connie, Hannah and Edward, for all their support and patience. And finally, thanks to everyone at Frances Lincoln for helping us to make *Go Wild* a reality.

For more information, see www.goingwild.net